CURSES!

WHY
CLEVELAND SPORTS FANS
DESERVE TO BE
MISERABLE

CURSES!

WHY
CLEVELAND SPORTS FANS
DESERVE TO BE
MISERABLE

**A Lifetime of Tough Breaks, Bad Luck,
Goofs, Gaffes, and Blunders**

TIM LONG

GRAY & COMPANY, PUBLISHERS
CLEVELAND

To Hal Lebovitz.
If there is such a thing as a Cleveland curse,
Hal was a blessing that helped us endure it.

Gray & Company, Publishers
1588 E. 40th St.
Cleveland, OH 44103-2302
www.grayco.com

ISBN 1-59851-018-5
Printed in the United States of America
First printing

INTRODUCTION

"Only in Cleveland . . ."

That's the lament, said with a sigh, used by our town's sports fans to explain the unexplainable. Why was Brian Sipe's pass intercepted by Oakland's Mike Davis in the 1980 playoffs, thus ending the magic of the Kardiac Kids? Why did Frank Lane trade our Indians' hero Rocky Colavito in 1960? Why couldn't Craig Ehlo block "The Shot" of Michael Jordon in the 1989 NBA play-offs? Why couldn't Ernie Davis have lived to run with Jim Brown in the Browns' backfield of the 1960s?

Our list of woes is endless, replete with bad trades, front office mistakes, personal tragedies, and various defeats snatched from the jaws of victory. Are we cursed? Probably not, but it often seems that way and it's a convenient catch-all for helping us deal with our fate.

Les Levine, Cleveland's sportscaster extraordinaire, has a simple approach to dealing with Cleveland's schizoid sports scene. "You've got to understand that we'll never, ever win. That makes it easier. We're allowed to get close and we did. But then there was Jose Mesa."

In his June 28, 2005, column, the *Plain Dealer's* Bill Livingston noted that, in Cleveland, "mistakes are the fans' meat, a 'curse' their potatoes, and victimization their approach to life." He aptly labeled Cleveland's defeatism as "the worst lake effect." Upon his arrival in Cleveland, even Phil Savage, the Browns' new general manager, observed, "There is a 'woe is me, run for the hills mentality' that seems to permeate Cleveland in general!" Sad, but true. Disappointment, absurdity, and tragedy make us feel alone and tragically unique but, hey, we're all in this together. What's that old saying from the 1980s t-shirts: "Cleveland . . . You Gotta Be Tough?" That's what we try to be, but sometimes it's hard to maintain the façade.

Terry Pluto, the award-winning *Akron Beacon Journal* sportswriter, says "I think our heartbreaks stand out because we've had so few big games to begin with, and we've come up short. Call it what you will, a curse, whatever . . . it is sad, and sometimes it seems a bit pathetic."

When you total up the seasons of the Browns, Indians, Cavaliers, and NHL Barons (for two seasons) since the Browns won an NFL crown in 1964, we've suffered through a combined 114* seasons with no major sports championships.

The famous columnist Heywood Broun once wrote, "The tragedy of life is not that man loses but that he almost wins." That about sums up professional sports in Cleveland.

Kenny Roda, whose sports talk show airs daily on WKNR Radio, recalls taking his son to see the Cavaliers play the Washington Wizards and Michael Jordan. With the Cavs ahead and just seconds on the clock, he told his son, watch—the Wizards will inbound the ball to Jordan, who will knock down the winning jump shot. "Because that's what happens in Cleveland," Roda said. And of course it did. "Jordan nailed the jumper as time expired. My son Cameron turned and looked at me in total disbelief. I said, 'Son, this is Cleveland sports. Learn to live with it.'"

We are the city that's divided by a crooked river that once caught fire. But one thing that seems to unite us is our sports, especially "our" Browns, "our" Indians, and "our" Cavaliers. If Cleveland could ever enter a psychiatrist's office and be put on the couch, imagine the purging of its collective sports misery— the absurd, the ugly, the insults . . . It's all in there waiting to be released.

"Cleveland, the doctor will see you now."

---

* Call it 117 if you want to count the three years, 1996–1998, when the Browns weren't playing in Cleveland.

WHY DO <u>YOU</u> FEEL CURSED?

Everyone's list will be different, but there's bound to be common ground among Cleveland sports fans regarding why we feel so darn cursed or unlucky or victimized by circumstances. Here's my list of 13—meant to start discussion and debate, not serve as the final word. The topic is Cleveland sports misery . . . discuss!

1. Art Modell's move of the Browns (1995)

2. Game Seven (1997)

3. "The Drive" (1986)

4. The trade of Rocky Colavito (1960)

5. "Red Right 88" (1980)

6. "The Shot" (1989)

7. The injury to Indians pitcher Herb Score (1957)

8. The trade of Paul Warfield (1970)

9. The loss of pitchers Steve Olin and Tim Crews (1993)

10. The trade of Ron Harper (1989)

11. The sale of the Indians to Nick Mileti instead of George Steinbreener (1972)

12. The tragic death of Ernie Davis (1963)

13. The Pitch That Killed: Ray Chapman (1920)

CURSES!

WHY CLEVELAND SPORTS FANS DESERVE TO BE MISERABLE

THE DRIVE

Did you just cringe when you read those two words? Did you close your eyes for a second and contemplate skipping this section? Because there is no more angst-filled description of a Browns game than "The Drive."

The Browns were confident of a trip to the Super Bowl before the 1986 AFC Championship game against the Denver Broncos, and it seemed a certainty with only 5:32 left to go in the game. Cleveland had just scored on a 48-yard touchdown pass from Bernie Kosar to Brian Brennan to go up 20-13. Now Denver was planted on their two-yard line with 98 yards to go for a tie. Then Denver was at the Cleveland 40-yard line facing a second down and 10 yards to go with 1:52 remaining. Elway was then sacked for an eight-yard loss by defensive tackle Dave Puzzuoli. How much more promising could it be? California dreamin' (as in Pasadena, site of that year's Super Bowl) swept away the iciness of Cleveland Municipal Stadium. The Broncos were third and 18 at midfield, with less than two minutes to go, and they needed a touchdown to tie. From the packed home crowd to the 60 million NBC television viewers, the consensus had the Browns taking this one from the Broncos.

HOW MUCH MORE PROMISING COULD IT BE?

Alas, Denver did tie it, and Elway's march to paydirt was memorialized in the damning phrase known simply as, "The Drive." Cleveland coach Marty Schottenheimer said after the game, "We had them third and 18, but they got the first down. There were others, but that [play] may have been the most important."

Thrust into overtime, the Browns won the toss and would own the pigskin first. Surely a Mark Mosely field goal could win this in OT, just as it had a week before in the playoff game against the New York Jets. The Browns began their drive at their 30-yard line, with Kosar forced to run for two yards. A six-yard pass to Brennan made it third down and two yards at the 38-yard line. What follows has got to be one of the Browns' most poorly conceived plays with the money on the line. The Browns needed two yards. They had a bruising fullback in Kevin Mack, who thundered for 3.8 yards per carry in 1986 and an amazing five yards per carry in 1985. The play? An inside off-tackle run by utility halfback Herman Fontenot. The result? No gain. Fotenot's worth was as a pass receiver, not a runner. Mack, who outweighed the 198-pound Fontenot by 27 pounds and was built, well, like a Mack truck, did not get the call for two of the most precious yards in Browns' history. Chances are good the Browns could have moved into position for the game-winning field goal. Instead, they punted, and Elway engineered a 50-yard drive, enabling kicker Rich Karlis to boot the heart-stabbing three-pointer that turned the California dream into a Red-Right 88 flashback.

Schottenheimer told his team in the locker room to hold their heads high and that this team "would be back." And so they would—one year later—to face the same Broncos, only this time in Denver. As much as that bit of news may have lifted the team's spirit on January 11, 1987, it was better that the Browns not have that glimpse into their future.

37 seconds too long

COLAVITO STUNNED BY LANE TRADE

HE KNOCKED THE ROCK

This is the queen mother of all bad Cleveland baseball trades, the horror of which still lives to this day. This trade would even spawn a phrase that explains more than 30 years of bad Indians baseball: the curse of Rocky Colavito. Rocky was a product of Cleveland's farm system who played for the big league Indians from 1955–1959 and again in 1965–1967. With his powerful bat, rifle right arm, and good looks, Rocky quickly won the hearts of fans. To them, he could do no wrong, as evidenced by the oft repeated phrase, "Don't knock the Rock." Yet on April 17, 1960, Cleveland's general manager, Frank "The Trader" Lane, pulled off a deal with Detroit Tigers' president William DeWitt that sent Colavito to the Tigers in exchange for Harvey Kuenn, the 1959 American League batting champ. Rocky was a power hitter; Kuenn hit singles and doubles for a higher average. Rocky was younger than Kuenn by three years and had the edge defensively, but, more significantly, Colavito was and remains one of the most popular Indians players ever.

Why did all of Cleveland take the trade so hard? Here's what *Cleveland Plain Dealer* sports editor Gordon Cobbledick wrote the day after the trade: "Many are aware of Rocky's limitations. They know he is an indifferent outfielder. They know he is a slow and uninspired base runner. They know he is capable of long spells when his bat is a feeble instrument. But they love him because he is Rocky Colavito! No more than a half dozen players in the history of

Fans Enraged

Cleveland baseball have been accorded the hero worship he enjoys. Rocky was our boy."

Indians pitcher Jim "Mudcat" Grant put it best when he said, "You want to know why Lane traded Rocky? That's easy. Lane was an idiot."

T.S. STANDS FOR "TOO STUPID"

If ever there was a true Cleveland sports embarrassment, Ted Stepien is it. Stepien started out as the owner of Nationwide Advertising and the Cleveland Competitors major league softball team. As the whole country would witness, it was a big jump, from owner of the Cleveland Competitors to that of the Cleveland Cavaliers. Too big, it turned out.

Just before the start of the 1980 NBA season, Stepien bought the Cleveland Cavaliers from original owner Nick Mileti, and truly dark days befell professional basketball in Cleveland. Stepien was unpredictable and inept, as evidenced by his goofy publicity stunts and irresponsible trades of draft picks in the early 1980s for questionable talent. The NBA was so outraged at Stepien's moves they created what has become known as the "Stepien Rule," which prohibits a team from trading future first-round picks in consecutive years. What an honor!

And who can forget the Cavaliers' cheerleaders named after the egotistical owner himself . . . the Teddy Bears. The Cavaliers had four coaches in one season, tying an NBA record set by the old Toronto Huskies in 1947.

Away from the world of pro basketball, Stepien was no better at controlling himself. In 1980 he sponsored a publicity stunt that injured two pedestrians on Public Square when softballs were dropped from the 52nd floor of the Terminal Tower.

After three years of the Stepien insanity, both on and off the court, the NBA basically forced the sale of the Cavaliers to an ownership group that would actually provide some adult supervision. The Gund brothers, Gordon and George, came to the rescue and purchased the Cavaliers for $20 million in 1983, just as Stepien was trying to move the team to Toronto, where he intended to name them the Toronto Towers.

> **BACKGROUND:**
>
> The March 15, 1983, broadcast of the *Sportsline* radio show on WWWE:
>
> Host Pete Franklin: "I think the NBA has involved itself by its actions suggesting that TS is more stupid than any other man in the history of sports."
>
> Caller: "That man's a moron!"

But the most entertaining episode of the Stepien era has to be his feud with sports-radio talker Pete Franklin. Franklin hosted the *Sportsline* radio show on Cleveland radio station WWWE, (now WTAM), in the 1970s and 1980s. Franklin was constantly on Stepien's case, insulting him every chance he got. For those who remember Pete Franklin, that was normal behavior. He insulted everyone. Here's one of his diatribes on the hapless Stepien, delivered in March 1983: "Other than being a certifiable

Stepien listening to offers to move Cavs to Toronto

CURSES!

nut and pathological liar, there's probably nothing wrong with the guy. He's an infestment, a cancer, that has screwed up the league, has escalated salaries and is responsible for everything from venereal disease to whooping cough." Franklin went on to say the NBA considered Stepien "too stupid to operate" the franchise. From then on, Franklin referred to Stepien as simply "TS," or "Too Stupid."

Stepien filed a defamation of character suit against Franklin that was heard in Cuyahoga County Common Pleas court by Judge Bert Griffin. Griffin's opinion stated: "Franklin's diatribe consisted of the common language of a tavern or locker room sports outburst transferred to the airwaves . . . such radio dialogue cannot be regarded as 'atrocious and intolerable in a civilized community' however much one might prefer a different public style." Griffin found no damages for the plaintiff Stepien and ordered him to pay court costs. If asked at the time, most Cleveland fans would probably have regarded Stepien himself as "atrocious and intolerable in a civilized community," based on his near destruction of the Cavaliers.

NO TRICKS UP HIS SLEEVE

When he was named the first head coach of the expansion Cleveland Cavaliers in 1970, Bill Fitch knew what he was signing on for. He told the media early in his tenure, **"Remember, the name's Fitch, not Houdini."** The Cavs went 15-67 their first year and a combined 84-162 over the next three seasons.

DUBIOUS DRAFT

MAD DOG IN A MEAT MARKET

Sending an All-Pro player and your first two draft picks to another team in exchange for their first pick is a high price to pay for an unproven college player. But if that player can really play like a "mad dog in a meat market," it's worth it. If he doesn't, well, you have a whopping draft bust on your hands.

In the 1987 NFL draft, the Browns traded All-Pro linebacker Chip Banks plus their first- and second-round picks for the San Diego Chargers' higher first- and second-round picks. They used the first-round selection on Mike Junkin, a 6'-3", 230-pound linebacker from Duke University. Pro scouts touted his great potential as a starting linebacker in the NFL, even though he suffered a severe knee injury in 1985. Junkin did not sign a contract with the Browns until August 10, 1987, missing valuable training camp time. A wrist injury in 1987 cost him most of his rookie season. The 1988 season was cut short by a knee injury. In 1989 he was traded to the Kansas City Chiefs and was out of pro football by the end of the season, never to return.

The choice of Junkin ranks as one of the Browns' worst draft picks; it cost them dearly. Gone was four-time Pro-Bowler Chip Banks, who finished his 10-year NFL career with the Indianapolis Colts in 1992. Browns coach Marty Schottenheimer, a much better game coach than talent evaluator, was enamored with Junkin. But hitching the Browns' wagon to Junkin's star meant Schottenheimer disregarded the talent of defensive tackle Jerome Brown (two Pro-Bowl selections), linebacker Shane Conlan (three Pro-Bowl selections), and defensive back Rod Woodson (11 Pro-Bowl selections), all of whom were available when Junkin was picked. Now that's a real draft bust!

PRO SCOUTS TOUTED HIS GREAT POTENTIAL.

THE WORST TEAM IN BASEBALL HISTORY

In a 2003 article, *Sports Illustrated* ranked the precursor to the Cleveland Indians—the Spiders—as the worst team in baseball. Admitting that baseball statistics in 1899 don't amount to much, *SI* was swayed by the Spiders' 20-134 record (.130 winning percentage) and the circumstances under which they operated. The Spiders went 81-68 in 1898, but then their owner purchased the St. Louis Browns and, thinking the Brwons had the better chance to win, sent the nine best players on the Spiders to St. Louis—including pitcher Cy Young. Cleveland lost 40 of their final 41 games. They attracted 6,088 fans for the entire year. The Spiders would have had a 21-133 record, but they choked during a game in June, squandering a 10-1 ninth inning lead.

WHAT TIME WAS IT?

"I went through Cleveland once and it was closed."

Jay Johnston, journeyman outfielder who played with eight major league teams from 1966–1985.

WORLD SERIES DROUGHT

The Tribe ranks just behind the city of Chicago's Cubs and White Sox in enduring the most years since their last World Series Championship. We can lament our 56-year drought but keep in mind something former L.A. Dodgers manager Tommy Lasorda once said. "The best possible thing in baseball is winning the World Series. The second best thing is losing the World Series." Some teams haven't even had the chance to lose a World Series. The problem is, once you've lost one, you don't ever want to lose another.

WORLD SERIES DROUGHTS (through 2004 season)

TEAM	SERIES WINS	SERIES LOSSES	LAST TITLE	YRS. W/OUT A TITLE
Chicago Cubs	2	8	1908	96 years
Chicago White Sox	2	2	1917	87 years
Cleveland Indians	2	3	1948	56 years
San Francisco Giants	0	3		47 years
(New York Giants)	5	9	1954*	
Houston Astros	0	0		43 years
San Diego Padres	0	2		36 years
Washington Nationals (Montreal)	0	0		36 years*
Milwaukee Brewers	0	1		35 years
Texas Rangers	0	0		33 years
Pittsburgh Pirates	5	2	1979	25 years
Philadelphia Phillies	1	4	1980	24 years
St. Louis Cardinals	9	7	1982	22 years
Baltimore Orioles	3	4	1983	21 years
Detroit Tigers	4	5	1984	20 years
Kansas City Royals	1	1	1985	19 years
New York Mets	2	2	1986	18 years
Los Angeles Dodgers	5	4	1988	16 years
(Brooklyn Dodgers)	1	8	1955*	
Oakland Athletics	4	2	1989	15 years
(Philadelphia Athletics)	5	3	1930*	
Cincinnati Reds	5	4	1990	14 years
Minnesota Twins	2	1	1991	13 years
Colorado Rockies	0	0		13 years
Toronto Blue Jays	2	0	1993	11 years
Atlanta Braves	1	4	1995	9 years
(Milwaukee Braves)	1	1	1957*	
(Boston Braves)	1	1	1914*	
Tampa Bay Devil Rays	0	0		7 years
New York Yankees	26	13	2000	4 years
Arizona Diamondbacks	1	0	2001	3 years
L.A. (Anaheim) Angels	1	0	2002	2 years
Florida Marlins	2	0	2003	1 year
Boston Red Sox	6	4	2004	

Franchise Relocations

CURSES!

Sports Illustrated Cover Jinx

RYAN SHOULDERS HEAVY LOAD

On January 4, 1965, Browns quarterback Frank Ryan appeared on the sports weekly magazine cover passing the football, in the Browns victory over the Baltimore Colts in the December 27, 1964, NFL Championship game. Did Ryan become jinxed as a result of his appearance on the cover? Weeks later, Ryan suffered a shoulder separation in the annual Pro Bowl all-star game that plagued him the rest of his career.

STILL WAITING

"About a year and a half or so after that World Series, a guy asked me how long it took me to get over that last game. I told him, **'As soon as it happens, I'll let you know.'**"

—*Mike Hargrove, Indians manager, on Game Seven of the 1997 World Series.*

SUPER BOWL-LESS

Here's how the Browns stack up against the other NFL teams in Super Bowl appearances. The Browns are one of eight NFL teams never to make it to the ultimate game. Perhaps the Browns need to be heeding the advice of former Houston Oilers coach Bill Peterson who said, "Men, I want you just thinking of one word all season. One word and one word only—Super Bowl."

SUPER BOWL RECORDS (through 2004)

TEAM	APPEARANCES	WON	LOST
Dallas Cowboys	8	5	3
Denver Broncos	6	2	4
San Francisco 49'ers	5	5	0
Pittsburgh Steelers	5	4	1
Oakland Raiders*	4	2	2
Washington Redskins	5	3	2
New England Patriots	5	3	2
Miami Dolphins	5	2	3
Green Bay Packers	4	3	1
Buffalo Bills	4	0	4
Minnesota Vikings	4	0	4
New York Giants	3	2	1
St. Louis Rams*	2	1	1
Baltimore Colts*	2	1	1
Kansas City Chiefs	2	1	1
Cincinnati Bengals	2	0	2
Philadelphia Eagles	2	0	2
Baltimore Ravens	1	1	0
Chicago Bears	1	1	0
Los Angeles Raiders*	1	1	0
New York Jets	1	1	0
Tampa Bay Buccaneers	1	1	0
Atlanta Falcons	1	0	1
Carolina Panthers	1	0	1
Los Angeles Rams*	1	0	1
San Diego Chargers	1	0	1
Tennessee Titans	1	0	1
Arizona/St. Louis Cardinals	0		
Cleveland Browns	0		
Detroit Lions	0		
Houston Texans	0		
Indianapolis Colts*	0		
Jacksonville Jaguars	0		
New Orleans	0		
Seattle Seahawks	0		

* Franchise relocation

CURSES!

A Brown By Any Other Name . . .

In 1980, the Browns drafted a defensive end from the University
of Arizona by the name of Cleveland Crosby. How appropriate.
Crosby didn't pan out and never played in a regular season game
for the Browns. Could it have had something to do with his middle
name? His full name was Cleveland Pittsburgh Crosby.

THE CURSE OF BOBBY BRAGAN

Was Bobby Bragan the father of a string of Cleveland baseball
curses, sentencing the Cleveland Indians to 35 years of bad luck
with a few bright spots of mediocrity? Bragan denies it. Yet he
has made it into Cleveland sports lore as having put a hex on
the Cleveland Indians. From the Tribe's glory years between
1946 and 1957, the team had a winning percentage of .578 and
drew an average of 1.5 million fans per season. From 1958 to
1993, right before the Tribe moved into Jacobs Field, the Indians
struggled with a .468 winning percentage and attendance averaged 945,000 per season.

Hired to manage the Indians in January 1958 by general manager Hank Greenberg, Bragan never worked under Greenberg.
The infamous Frank "Trader" Lane replaced Greenberg only
a month after Bragan was hired, and in early July 1958, it was
Bragan's turn as Lane summoned him to his office after a 1-0
loss to the Boston Red Sox. "I don't know how we'll get along
without you, Bobby, but starting tomorrow, we're going to try,"
Lane said.

Once fired, rumor has it that Bragan put a curse on the Indians by walking out to the infield at old Cleveland Municipal Stadium, ripping out the second base bag, and declaring that no future Indians team would ever come close to a pennant.

In 1984, members of the Cleveland media brought a witch named Elizabeth from Salem, Massachusetts, to Cleveland Stadium for Opening Day. Her task was to lift the so-called Bragan curse. Making her way to the second base bag, Elizabeth

THE WITCH ANNOUNCED THE COMPLETE ERADICATION OF THE EVIL SPELL

chanted, incanted, and bantered her way to transforming the curse into good fortune. After collapsing on second base, she announced the complete eradication of Bragan's evil spell.

Two years later, Richard and David Jacobs bought the team. Then, a new stadium was built, and the Tribe appeared in two World Series in the 1990s. As Bragan describes it in his book, *You Can't Hit the Ball with the Bat on Your Shoulders,* "There's an ongoing rumor I put a curse on the Indians after Lane fired me. To this day, I get calls from Cleveland sportswriters and disc jockeys who ask if it's true. No, it isn't. I didn't need to hex the club. Having Frank Lane as its general manager was curse enough."

LIP SERVICE

STILL AFLOAT IN CLEVELAND

Although New York sportswriter Barney Nagler devoted most of his time to boxing and thoroughbred racing, he would offer opinions on other subjects in his column "On Second Thought," which appeared in the *New York Morning Telegraph* from 1950–1990. From the Big Apple, Barney took notice of Cleveland during some of our trying times and was moved to comment, **"The only difference between the Cleveland and the Titanic is that the Titanic had better restaurants."** Thanks, Barney!

DUBIOUS DRAFT

DISABLED DEJUAN

Guard Andre Miller was a solid pick for the Cleveland Cavaliers in the 1999 NBA Draft. He was described as the best pure point guard in the draft, a player who who could lead a team and play defense. The guard from Utah had three productive seasons for the Cavs when his agent informed the team that Miller would seek the maximum salary allowed under the NBA rules after his rookie contract expired. Unable to fit this within their budget, the Cavs shopped Miller to other teams.

To protect themselves, they selected Dejuan Wagner, a guard from Memphis, in the first round of the NBA Draft in June 2002. At 19, with only one year of college ball behind him, Wagner was mostly a business-move pick. Though described as "electrifying" in his one year at Memphis, he missed 59 percent of his field goal shots. In July, after the Cavs traded Miller to the Los Angeles Clippers, they looked to Wagner to eventually fill some big shoes. What he filled, instead, was a medical file. In his rookie season in 2002, he was sidelined with a bladder infection and played his first NBA game in late November. In March 2003, arthroscopic surgery on his right knee sidelined him for the rest of the year. He appeared in 47 games that year. In October 2003, he re-injured the same knee and had another surgical procedure. He played his first game of the 2003–2004 season on January 7 but missed more games with a sore right knee. He played in 44 games that season. In training camp for the 2004–2005 season, Wagner sprained his ankle in a preseason game. He finally played in November. In January 2005, Wagner was sidelined with colitis and was shut down for the year with his future uncertain. He played in 11 games for the Cavs that season. No wonder many fans consider this one of the most painful transactions in Cavs history.

TENNIS ANYONE?

At one point in its history, Cleveland was a focal point for world-class tennis as it hosted the women's Wightman Cup matches and the men's Davis Cup matches. The Wightman matches were competitions between the United States and Great Britain that have since evolved into the Fed Cup. In 1967, Cleveland drew a record-setting crowd of 10,000 to a Wightman match. The men's Davis Cup originally matched the United States against Great Britain but has grown into a truly international competition. The city was a regular venue for the more prestigious Davis Cup matches in the 1960s and 1970s, showing a knack for sponsorship and tournament organization.

Cleveland hosted the zone Davis matches in 1960 at the Cleveland Skating Cub. The 1964 and 1969 challenge round matches, and the Davis Cup final rounds in 1969, 1970, and 1973 were held at the Harold T. Clark tennis courts, named after the Cleveland philanthropist and tennis patron. Cleveland could have been the site for the first U.S. Open Tennis Tournament in 1968. But of course, it wasn't. What happened? As Bill Nichols wrote in the

CLEVELAND COULDN'T KEEP ITSELF IN THE GAME

August 8, 1968 edition of the *Plain Dealer*, "This is a tournament that almost came to Cleveland. New York, Cleveland, and Los Angeles bid for the first open and our city lost for one very important reason—no place to play."

There were great expectations for an exhibition tennis stadium to be built at the new Cleveland Racquet Club in 1969, but the project never materialized due to lack of financial support. While there was a brief volley of tennis tournament action with the Bonne Bell Cup in the early 1970s, Cleveland couldn't keep itself in the game to build on its tennis legacy, all because it couldn't build an appropriate facility for the events.

TOUGH LUCK

BOSTON MASSACRE

No one saw the Cleveland Indians as World Series contenders in 1999. Playoffs, yes, but conventional wisdom said the Tribe's pitching wasn't strong enough to carry them the whole way. Facing the Boston Red Sox in the American League Division Series, the Indians squeaked by in Game One at Jacobs Field by a score of 3-2. The victory was satisfying because it came at the expense of Boston ace Pedro Martinez, one of the most intimidating pitchers in baseball. Pedro lasted only four innings, removing himself from the game because of muscle spasms in his back. Tribe fans were giddy over the prospect. After the game, Indians third baseman Travis Fryman commented, "Anytime you face Pedro, he's tough. You look up there in the sixth inning and you don't see him out there, it gives you a little 'pick-me-up.'" The euphoria continued in Game Two when the Red Sox were clubbed 11-1 by the hard-hitting Indians, and it was off to Boston with a two-game advantage.

The Tribe's Game Three starter was right-hander Dave Burba, who was hurling a shutout through four innings, protecting a one run lead. But as tightness developed in Burba's right forearm, the same feeling began to sweep through the stomachs of Indians' fans every-

FROM THIS POINT ON, IT BECAME UGLY.

where. Burba was forced to leave the game, as manager Mike Hargrove went to Jaret Wright in an unplanned relief role. From this point on, it became ugly. Wright, Ricardo Rincon, and Sean DePaula gave up a total of nine runs in three innings, and the Tribe fell by a score of 9-3. Still up by a 2-1 edge in the playoff series, Cleveland could not anticipate what would happen the next day in Game Four. The 33,898 delirious Fenway Park fans witnessed a 23-7 bludgeoning of the hapless Indians. It was bad from the get-go. Bartolo Colon started the game on only three days rest from Game One in Cleveland; something he had never done before, and it showed in his wildness.

Back in the friendly confines of Jacobs Field, the Indians knew it was do-or-die time. Charles Nagy, who had won Game Two of the series, faced Bret Saberhagen. There was a real chance to salvage this series that had gone wrong. After three and a half innings, the game was locked in an 8-8 tie, and the Indians were determined to break it in the bottom of the fourth. The left-for-dead Pedro Martinez took the hill in the fourth inning and stymied the Tribe in the 4th, 5th, and 6th innings. What transpired in the Boston half of the seventh inning lends credence to a Cleveland baseball curse. Nomar Garciaparra, the 1999 American League batting champion, struck terror into the heart of manager Mike Hargrove. After Garciaparra homered in the first inning, Hargrove instructed Charles Nagy to intentionally walk him in the third inning, thus loading the bases. Stepping in the batter's box was left fielder Troy O'Leary, who was having a terrible series and had struck out in the first inning. O'Leary promptly deposited Nagy's first pitch into the right-center field stands and went into the Boston record books with the first postseason grand slam home run in club history. Slumping players can get lucky, and O'Leary did.

Deadlocked in the top of the seventh, reliever Paul Shuey was also told to give Nomar a free pass to first, now putting runners on first and second. Apparently Hargrove still feared Garciaparra more than he did the grand slamming O'Leary. But this was O'Leary's day, his season, his career, perhaps. Nicknamed "Yummy" by his teammates because he loved sweets, O'Leary sugarcoated a Paul Shuey offering into the Jacobs Field seats for a three-run homer that put the Bosox in the lead to stay. The final score was 12-8. Martinez held the Tribe scoreless for six innings. Cleveland was the victim of a Boston Massacre.

IT WAS BAD
FROM THE GET-GO.

BAD TRADE

THE LEGEND WHO GOT AWAY

Described as "poetry in motion" by his Miami Dolphins coach Don Shula, Paul Warfield is the Rocky Colavito of the Cleveland Browns. His trade in 1970 is a low point in the Browns' history.

A product of Warren, Ohio, and Ohio State University, Warfield was drafted in the first round of the 1964 NFL draft by the Browns. Warfield averaged a stunning 20.7 yards per catch in his 1964–1969 stint with the Browns. By the end of 1969, however, Browns quarterback Bill Nelsen was approaching 30 years of age and his knees were shot, so the Browns were looking to find his successor. They zeroed in on the 1969 Heisman Trophy runner-up and consensus All-American quarterback, Mike Phipps from Purdue University. To secure this strong-armed athlete, the Browns needed to move into the third spot of the first round in the 1970 draft. The Miami Dolphins owned the pick and were willing to part with it under one condition—the Browns give them wide receiver Paul Warfield in exchange. The Browns felt the demand was worth it and selected Phipps with the third pick of the draft.

Warfield, as well as the city of Cleveland, was rocked by the trade: "I was disappointed because I believed I had made a positive contribution to the team. I wasn't a troublemaker and I felt that wasn't the way to reward an employee who had done a good job." Phipps played seven unspectacular years in Cleveland and was traded to the Chicago Bears in 1977 for the Bears' 1978 first-round pick— which was a good thing since it was used to acquire tight end Ozzie Newsome. Phipps exited pro football after the 1981 season with 55 touchdown passes and 108 interceptions. Warfield caught 427

BROWNS TRADE WARFIELD

passes for 8,565 yards for a spectacular 20.1 yards per catch. He was named to eight Pro Bowls and five All-NFL teams and played on two Miami Super Bowl championship teams. He also made one other stop along the way . . . the Pro Football Hall of Fame in Canton, Ohio.

Coincidence or not, the Warfield trade signaled the beginning of a 10-year decline for the Browns, while the Miami Dolphins became the premier team in professional football. Former Browns linebacker Jim Houston said the trade "didn't make sense." He wasn't alone. In 1976, the Browns brought Warfield back to Cleveland. Although Warfield was happy to retire as a member of the Browns, his return, like Colavito's, was merely symbolic.

.... **ONLY IN CLEVELAND** ....

A Burning Issue

Gib Shanley was the radio voice of the Cleveland Browns from 1961–1984. But in November 1979, Gib gained notoriety for the stunt he pulled on an 11 o'clock news broadcast. A story had run on that evening's 6 o'clock news about an Iranian burning an American flag. Because this happened at the time American embassy employees in Iran were being held hostage, Shanley was outraged. The story was repeated at 11 o'clock, and when the camera switched to him, he had already grabbed a small Iranian flag that was on the news desk and set it afire with a lighter. Gib and the flaming flag were on air for 12 seconds, then viewers burned up the phone lines . . . with calls of support. As Shanley reflected years later in an interview with Debbie Hanson of clevelandseniors.com, "Today there would be lawsuits, a demand for a public apology and I'd be off the air, but things were different then. I had to promise not to do it again, but frankly, I suppose I would do it again today."

....

TOUGH
LUCK

FASTER THAN SANDY KOUFAX

There's a song by singer Terry Cashman called "The Ballad of Herb Score" that captures the essence of this Indians' tough luck story in song:

Then one night he took the mound
He was on his way to Cooperstown,
One pitch and history was changed
McDougald swung and Herb was shattered
Tried to come back but it never really mattered,
And that's why you never heard of Herbie Score.

Generations of Cleveland baseball fans have not only heard of Herb Score and his story, they feel they know Herb better than any other Tribesman. At 23 years old, this overpowering left-hander from Rosedale, New York, had already racked up impressive credentials. In 1955, Score won the American League Rookie of the Year Award and won 16 games. The following year he was a 20-game winner for the Tribe. In both seasons he led the American League in strikeouts. But on May 7, 1957, in a game against the Yankees at Cleveland Municipal Stadium, "history was changed." Score threw a low pitch to the Yankee's second batter of the game, Gil MacDougald, who sent a shot directly at Score, who was finishing his delivery. According to MacDougald, "The next thing I remember is watching Herb go down. All I recall seeing is blood." Score had been hit in the right cheekbone near his eye. Witnesses at the Stadium that night recall hearing a "sickening thud" and seeing their young phenom lying on the ground, not knowing how badly he was hurt. Cleveland newspaper headlines delivered the unfortunate news the following morning and everyone across Cleveland asked each other repeatedly: "Did you hear Herb Score was hit in the eye last night?" Score lay in a Cleveland hospital with his eyes covered for two weeks, wondering if he would have sight when the bandages came off. McDougald reportedly vowed to quit baseball if Score lost his sight.

SCORE HIT IN EYE BY LINE DRIVE

Score missed the remainder of the 1957 season but returned in 1958, going 2-3. While it was logical to conclude that Score's eye injury derailed his ride to Cooperstown, Score disputed that: "What happened is that I injured a tendon in my pitching arm at the beginning of the 1958 season and kept pitching. That was the problem." Some observers around the league maintained that Score naturally altered his delivery after the accident, and it became somewhat mechanical. Whatever the reasons, the route of Herb Score's career in baseball took a turn and he wound up in the Indians' broadcast booth, in television from 1964–1967 and on radio from 1968–1997. This is where the majority of Indians fans got to know Herb, his wit, and his unique, low-key style of calling a game. But the notion that he could have been the greatest left-hander of all time can never be erased. As former Indian great Tris Speaker said of Score, "If nothing happens to him, this kid has got to be the greatest."

Sports Illustrated Cover Jinx

FINAL SCORE

On May 30, 1955, Herb Score graced the cover of *Sports Illustrated* under the headline "Big New Indian." Just under two years later, he was struck in the face by a line drive off the bat of the Yankees' Gil MacDougald.

TOUGH LUCK

CARR IS SIDETRACKED

One of the classiest people to ever wear the Wine and Gold, Austin Carr, known as "AC," had greatness written over him when he finished his All-American college career at the University of Notre Dame in 1971. Drafted in the first round by the Cavaliers, Carr continued his scoring ways during his first three seasons in the NBA, averaging more than 20 points per game. But—tough luck—a knee injury in 1974 reduced his playing time and productivity and perhaps prevented his enshrinement in basketball's hall of fame. After his injury, Carr took up the duties of the Cavs' "sixth man," doing what was best for the team. Still, he endeared himself to Cleveland basketball fans, who voted him to the Cavaliers' 30th Anniversary all-time best Cavaliers team.

LIP SERVICE

OUT OF THE MOUTH OF BEN

In 2001, Browns rookie running back Ben Gay burst onto the Cleveland sports scene. Propelled by a meteoric Texas high school football career and despite an otherwise checkered past, Gay was a real piece of work. While speaking of his development as a young player in the NFL, Ben said, **"Trust me, I'm still at no peak. I'm just a rock on the bottom of Mount Saint Rushmore."** Gentle Ben was also famous for, **"I got nothin' against Christmas; it just comes at the wrong time of year."**

THE WAY THE SOCCER BALL BOUNCES

Professional soccer, Cleveland style, has been a tale of ups and downs since the original Cleveland Force was born in 1978. As one of the charter members of the MISL (Major Indoor Soccer League), the Force was a red-hot commodity in Cleveland at times during the 1980s. During the 1986 season, the Force won the Eastern Conference title in front of 20,176 fans at the Richfield Coliseum by beating the Minnesota Strikers. They clinched the Eastern Conference crown again in 1987 but were swept by the San Diego Sockers in the MISL title game. In July 1988, the Force and their mascot, Darth Vader, were vaporized and became only a memory.

In 1989, Cleveland received a new MSL (Major Soccer League) franchise known as the Cleveland Crunch, which lasted until 1992 when the Crunch joined the NPSL (National Professional Soccer League). The Crunch provided Cleveland with its first league championship titles since the 1964 Browns when they won the NPSL crowns in 1994, 1996, and 1999. But in August 2001 the NPSL was dissolved.

Refusing to die, the Crunch gained membership in the new MISL (Major Indoor Soccer League). One year later, soccer in Cleveland came full circle as the Crunch changed their name to . . . the Force. In the 2005 MISL title game, the Force fell to the Milwaukee Wave. Unfortunately, the Force may no longer be with Cleveland, as it and the MISL may not make it financially. Principal owner Richard Dietrich told the *Plain Dealer*, "I am saddened; truly saddened by exiting this business. I love soccer. I take no joy out of seeing this franchise go away."

"I am saddened; truly saddened by exiting this business. I love soccer. I take no joy out of seeing this franchise go away."

BAD TRADE

"THE NEXT LARRY BIRD"

The 1989 NBA draft was drawing near, so Cavaliers general manager Wayne Embry decided to quell rumors about possible trades involving his players. John "Hot Rod" Williams and former Miami of Ohio star Ron Harper were rumored to be part of draft-day dealings. "None of this stuff is true," Embry said. "There is nothing to either one. If there was any substance at all, I would say so . . . we are not shopping any of our key players." He forgot to add, "at this time."

In November 1989, just after the start of the NBA season, Embry sent Harper, a fast-rising star, plus two future first-round and a second-round draft picks to the Los Angeles Clippers for the negotiating rights to Duke University star Danny Ferry and the Clippers' Reggie Williams. But Ferry was playing in Italy, having told the Clippers he would never play for them. The Clippers did a masterful job of fleecing the Cavaliers in this trade. The Cavaliers waited until Ferry completed his fling in Italian basketball and signed him to a whopping 10-year, $34 million contract. Ferry was billed in some quarters as "the next Larry Bird," but other NBA scouts thought his defensive liabilities were covered up well while playing at Duke and would be exposed in the NBA. Cleveland paid a huge price to find out that Ferry's hype couldn't translate into star-quality in the NBA.

THE CLIPPERS DID A MASTERFUL JOB OF FLEECING THE CAVALIERS IN THIS TRADE.

Harper, of course, ended up being one of the league's better open court players and improved his game to where he became an important component of the Chicago Bulls' championship teams of 1996, 1997, and 1998. He finished his NBA career with 13,910 points (13.8 pts./game) and 4,309 rebounds. Ferry, on the other hand, ranks

Cavaliers trade Harper

as one of the Cavs' biggest draft busts, although he did gain the distinction of becoming the Cavaliers' leader in games played. He finished his NBA playing career with the San Antonio Spurs in 2002 with career total points of 6,439 (7.0 pts./game) and 2,550 rebounds.

Some Cleveland fans cringed when Danny Ferry returned to Cleveland in June 2005 as the Cavaliers new general manager. The ghost of the Danny Ferry trade still haunts the Cavs faithful, and they were wondering what kind of GM they were getting. At his introductory press conference, the ex-Cavalier was reminded of the trade that sent NBA star Ron Harper to the Clippers for him. One reporter asked Ferry if he would have made that deal. Ferry laughed out loud and replied, "No comment."

Tragedy

CLEVELAND'S OWN "NATURAL"

The loss of talented power hitter Tony Horton was not due to a bad trade or a botched salary negotiation. Sadly, the story of this handsome Californian goes deeper than just the game of baseball. Horton came to Cleveland on June 4, 1967, from the Boston Red Sox in exchange for pitcher Gary Bell. He had played parts of three big-league seasons for the Red Sox after being signed as an amateur free agent in 1962. During spring training in 1963, the Red Sox's hitting instructor, Ted Williams, commented that Horton "is a natural" and suggested that no one mess with his swing. Those are some heavy words from one of baseball's greatest hitters.

Horton was an intense competitor, and during the 1969 season he batted a solid .278 with 27 home runs and 93 runs batted-in while playing first base. During the winter of 1969–1970, Horton and his father began negotiating a new contract with Tribe manager Alvin Dark. Dark was using recently acquired first baseman Ken Harrelson as leverage to stonewall the Hortons and force Tony to accept the Tribe's terms. Three weeks into spring training, Horton reluctantly agreed to the Tribe's terms. As luck would have it, Ken Harrelson, Dark's ace-in-the-hole, broke a leg the next day!

The life of Tony Horton turned even more unfortunate as the 1970 season unfolded. The timing of Harrelson's injury, insulting comments about Horton's fielding abilities made by Alvin Dark, and the fans' negative reaction to his holdout provided Horton with the motivation to prove everyone wrong. But the unwinding of Tony Horton became more and more evident as he was squeezed in a vice of his own making: he would not allow himself to fail.

In a game at Yankee Stadium on June 24, 1970, Horton faced the Yanks' left-hander Steve Hamilton, who occasionally threw slow, soft pitches dubbed "floaters." Horton swung wildly at the floaters until he lamely popped out. What happened next seemed like a joke. Horton crawled back to the dugout on his hands and knees, while both dugouts laughed at his failure to hit the junk-ball pitches.

In subsequent games, teammates began noticing Horton's fixed gaze and his failure to even crack a smile upon hitting a home run. By August 28, 1970, the Indians lost their 25-year-old slugger. He had simply "checked out." During a doubleheader against the California Angels he showed up but did not suit-up for either game. At some point during the two-game set, Horton left Municipal Stadium, never to play professional baseball again.

Hospitalization in Cleveland was followed by more treatment at his home in Santa Monica, California, which caused him to miss spring training in 1971. But everyone knew he wouldn't be back. He eventually settled into a quieter, less stressful life in California. When Horton left the Tribe, he was hitting .269 with 17 home runs and 59 runs batted-in. Not bad production for the Indians, but never good enough for Tony Horton.

"I started my life over and baseball is not a part of it."

—Tony Horton

DUBIOUS DRAFT

WHO'S DOING THE SCOUTING?

After the 1953 season, the Browns began looking for a successor to quarterback Otto Graham, their eventual Hall-of-Famer. On January 28, 1954, the Browns drew the No. 1 bonus pick in the NFL draft and quickly selected the nation's leading collegiate passer of 1953, Stanford's Bobby Garrett. Cleveland Browns coach Paul Brown knew his stuff. Garrett was projected to be the team's eventual starter after a few seasons learning from the sidelines. This pick, it turns out, was wasted. But it could have been worse.

Crafty Paul Brown soon realized his pick wasn't what he'd planned on and traded Garrett to the Green Bay Packers for two players who had just been called for two years of military service. Had Paul Brown lost his mind?

Green Bay fullback Fred Cone later explained, "Garrett stuttered. He couldn't get the plays out in the huddle. We had to crack him on the back so he could spit out the play." Garrett didn't play much for the Packers and in 1957 was traded back to the Browns. He never played a game for Cleveland and was soon out of football for good.

LIP SERVICE

> ## "The only good thing about [playing in] Cleveland is you don't have to make road trips there."
>
> —*Richie Scheinblum, Cleveland Indians outfielder (1965, 1967–1969)*

WHAT THIS TOWN NEEDS IS
A GOOD TEN-CENT BEER!

In 1974, attendance at Tribe games averaged just shy of 8,000 fans per game. So it wasn't surprising that management tried to devise special attractions (how about a competitive team?) that would help draw an audience. One of those promotions did indeed draw fans. Unfortunately, it also drew trouble—and led to a debacle. It became the most disgraceful moment in Cleveland sports history.

On June 4, 1974, the Texas Rangers rode into Cleveland for a three-game series. The Tribe had met the Rangers a week earlier in Arlington, Texas, and during one of those games, a fight broke out between the teams. The Texas fans felt obligated to participate, since they were chugging down discounted beer that night, and showered the Indians' players with cheap suds and foul language.

The Indians reciprocated on June 4 with "Ten Cent Beer Night." Although the Rangers and Indians players had cooled off, Cleveland fans apparently were out to settle the score. They loudly booed Rangers manager Billy Martin when he delivered the lineup card to the umpires before the game. Returning to the dugout, "Billy the Kid" tipped his hat and blew kisses to the crowd of 25,000 (noticeably larger than average). The crowd was incensed.

During the first inning, several smoke bombs were set off in the outfield stands. The second inning saw a rather Rubenesque but scantily clad young lady run onto the field to kiss umpire Nester Chylak. In the fourth inning, Tom Grieve of the Rangers hit his second home run of the night, motivating a Cleveland streaker to join him on the field as he rounded the bases. A father and son stood up and mooned the field from the center field stands in the fifth. By the seventh inning, the fans had become so

Stadium beer night fans riot, ending Indians' rally in forfeit

drunk they were jumping from the right-field stands onto the field to pester Rangers' outfielder Jeff Burroughs. All this occurred against the backdrop of firecrackers, smoke bombs, and thrown beer cups.

Finally, in the ninth inning, the wayward promotion hit its nadir and dove into infamy. The ratio of fans-to-security personnel was a mismatch. The police did their best to escort drunken fans from the field, but when the Tribe tied the game in the bottom of the ninth, things got plain ugly. A fan engaged in a brief tussle with Burroughs, trying to make off with the 6'-2", 200-pound-outfielder's mitt. As Burroughs chased the fan, a posse of inebriated patrons surrounded the outfielder. Billy Martin ran toward right field, waving a broken bat in an attempt to rescue his player. Rangers' players followed their valiant manager; even Cleveland players ran to rescue their Texas counterparts, but the tragic result was thousands of fans pouring onto the field.

Amidst the mayhem, beer and blood flowed freely. Indians pitcher Tom Hilgendorf was hit over the head with a chair, umpire Nester Chylak was bloodied when hit in the head by a rock, and fans suffered cuts and bloody noses as they fought with the players and each other. As both teams finally reached the safety of their respective dugouts, Chylak ordered the game a forfeit—in the record books it shows the Rangers receiving credit for the win by a score of 9-0. It was only the fourth American League forfeit in history. For Cleveland, it was an unqualified embarrassment and yet another mistake by the lake.

> *"We went as far as we could go, but you can't pull back uncontrollable beasts. The last time I saw animals like that was in the zoo."*
>
> —Umpire Netser Chylak

Tragedy

STATIC ON THE AIRWAVES

Cleveland fans lost a real treasure with the untimely death in 1994 of Nev Chandler, the radio voice of the Cleveland Browns for the previous nine years. Nev's resume also included Tribe radio broadcasts and WEWS Channel 5 sportscasting. Whether it was Nev's mimicking of ABC sportscaster Howard Cosell or his patented descriptions of thrilling Browns games ("It's science fiction time at Cleveland Municipal Stadium!"), Nev was the consummate professional and a good guy.

COACH MACKEY CRACKS THE BIG TIME

Mention Cleveland sports and you'll immediately get an earful about the Indians, the Browns, and the Cavaliers. Cleveland is pretty much known for pro teams, but other cities like Columbus, Philadelphia, Milwaukee, and Chicago have garnered attention within college basketball ranks as well. Columbus has the Buckeyes; Philly's Villanova has an NCAA championship, as does Milwaukee's Marquette and Chicago's DePaul. That's why the 1986 saga of the basketball Vikings of Cleveland State University captivated not only the citizens of Cleveland but also the country's March Madness freaks as well. Fans seem to get behind the underdog, and there was no dog that was as under as CSU. Described as that "small commuter school," CSU and its Vikings were an unknown quantity as they received a bid to the NCAA championship tournament. The Vikings were good, but the stock phrase outside of Northeast Ohio was still, "Cleveland who?"

College basketball popularity in Cleveland began to change when Kevin Mackey, the cocky Irishman with the broad "Baahstan" accent, left an assistant's job at Boston College and took over at 22nd and Euclid Avenue in 1983. Fans began to witness the "run and stun" style of basketball, where CSU would exhaust opponents with a withering full-court press and a fast-motion offense. In his first season at the helm, Mackey coached CSU to a 14-16 record, a marked improvement from the previous season's 20 losses. The following season the Vikings kicked into high gear with a 21-8 record and an Association of Mid-Continent Universities (AMCU) conference championship. At season's end, Mackey found himself with AMCU Coach of the Year honors.

The winter of 1986 saw Mackey and the Vikings grab the attention of college basketball fans everywhere. The team won all 15 home games, rode a 12-game winning streak at the end of the year, finished 29-4, and claimed another AMCU conference championship. Mackey repeated as the AMCU Coach of the Year. Yet these are but footnotes to the highlight of that year: CSU earned an at-large bid to the NCAA East regional tournament. The consensus of the city was typical Cleveland: winning a tournament game would be great, but it was enough to just get the invitation.

Mackey and some of his star players, however, weren't from Cleveland. They had a different take on things. On March 14, 1986, the David of Cleveland State was matched against the Goliath of Bobby Knight's Indiana University. CSU outlasted the nationally ranked Hoosiers by a score of 83-

IT EARNED THE VIKINGS INSTANT NOTORIETY.

79 in the first round of tournament play. It was a stunning upset that was broadcast nationally on cable channel ESPN. It earned the Vikings instant notoriety. After the game, John Wooden, former UCLA coach, commented that Cleveland State played basketball the way the game was supposed to be played.

Next up was St. Joseph's University, the small Philadelphia

college with a history of fine teams and tournament experience. CSU grounded the Hawks 75-69 to advance to the Sweet Sixteen of the tournament. A win against the U.S. Naval Academy in the third round would advance the Vikings to the Elite Eight and then, maybe, just maybe . . . The nation was noticing, and the city was in love with the Vikings. What looked like another stunning upset against Navy and their great center David Robinson turned into disappointment as Robinson scored the winning basket with 5 seconds left. Navy-71; Cleveland State-70.

Cleveland collegiate basketball rolled with the momentum from that winning season and started to establish itself on the local and national scene. In the next two seasons, CSU finished with records of 25-8 (1986–1987) and 22-8 (1987–1988) with trips to the collegiate National Invitational Tournament (NIT). Then followed a setback. During the 1988–1989 season, the NCAA placed the program on two years' probation for recruiting violations; the season record dipped to 16-12. The 1989–1990 season was mediocre at 15-13, but the program would be coming off probation and eligible for tournament play once more. On July 11, 1990, Kevin Mackey inked a new two-year contract. Could this mark the return to tournament-quality basketball?

No.

Two days later Cleveland Police were tipped off that Coach Mackey was somewhere he shouldn't have been—in an East

CSU's Mackey faces DUI charge
Basketball coach arrested near suspected drug house

Side Cleveland crack house. Television crews arrived and put a full court press on the coach as they filmed him leaving the house with a prostitute. Days later, Mackey was fired.

Had Mackey soared too far, too fast? In a January 2004 interview with *USA Today,* Mackey seems to confirm this: "They wrote in the paper that I was the King of Cleveland and a civic treasure. My money didn't matter and everything was free. And you start to believe the bull . . . So you know, I was a little younger, ran the street at night, that energy, that adrenaline and the whole thing . . . I'd be in places at 3 or 4 in the morning, my big car out front, with all the bad guys." Addiction brought Kevin Mackey down, and so went the dreams of a hopeful city that had once tasted sweetness.

"July 13, 1990, was the day Cleveland State basketball died."

Joe Maxse, *Cleveland Plain Dealer* reporter and CSU alumni.

TOUGH LUCK

CHONES'S BAD BREAK

The 1975–1976 Cavaliers basketball season will forever be known as the "Miracle of Richfield." The Cavaliers posted a 49-33 record and made it to the first round of the NBA playoffs against the Washington Bullets. In the deciding Game Seven of this series, Dick Snyder made a miraculous shot over the Bullets' Phil Chenier to seal the victory. It ranks as one of the Cavaliers' most dramatic moments. Those that were at the Coliseum that night recall the near-deafening sound of the crowd. Three of the four Cavs' victories were decided by two points, one point, and one point.

As the Cavaliers were practicing their match-up with the Boston Celtics in the Eastern Conference finals, tragedy struck. Leading

Chones out of playoffs

scorer and team center Jim Chones broke a bone in his right foot that would shelve him for the crucial series. That meant much more playing time for 34-year-old back-up center Nate Thurmond, who would would face the NBA's Most Valuable player, Dave Cowens. Chones said that he could "live with something like this. It's the rest of the guys I really feel sorry for." But the Cavs refused to feel sorry for themselves as they fought valiantly in the best-of-seven series, losing the first two games to the Celtics in Boston, winning two at home, but losing two more in Boston.

Always ready to offer deadpan comic relief, Cavs' coach Bill Fitch said before the start of the series with Boston, "Really, the pressure is on the Celtics now. They're going to have to go around and say they got beat by Cleveland when they didn't have Jim Chones."

BAD TRADE

FRANK LANE, CLUELESS AS EVER

Even the casual baseball fan knows Roger Maris. He broke Babe Ruth's single-season 60-home-run mark as a member of the New York Yankees. Yet if one pages through a baseball card catalog and happens upon the *Topps* 1958 collection, Roger Maris appears on his rookie card attired in the gray flannel "away" uniform of the Cleveland Indians. (One would also learn that a PSA Gem Mint 10 graded Maris rookie card could grab between $4,000–$5,000 today.)

Maris was special in that he was "home-grown" within the Tribe's farm system after signing a $15,000-per-year contract out of high school. After four years in the minors, Roger hit 14 home runs and 51 RBI for the big-league Tribe in 1957.

Alas, Maris played about two months for the Indians in 1958 before being shipped to Kansas City by Cleveland's general manager Frank Lane, along with two other players, for first baseman Vic Power and shortstop Woodie Held. In 1958, Roger's home run production doubled to 28, and his RBI total climbed to 80. In 1959, he was selected for the American League All-Star team. After the 1959 season, the Kansas City Athletics traded Maris to the New York Yankees. His career in the vaunted pinstripes included the American League Most Valuable Player (MVP) award in 1960 and 1961, four trips to the All-Star game, and a record 61 home runs hit in 1961. Enough said!

Once, when Frank Lane's days as Cleveland's GM were through, Lane casually mentioned to a local sportswriter that the trade of Maris for Power and Held was one of the better deals he made for the Tribe. Hmm, wonder what Vic Power's and Woodie Held's rookie cards are going for these days?

EVERYONE LOVES A PARADE

It's great to get behind your home team and celebrate their accomplishments. Granted, the Indians' loss to the Atlanta Braves in the 1995 World Series came 41 years after the Tribe last appeared in the Fall Classic. But, please. Let's have a parade for a champion, not a runner-up. In true "second place is good enough" spirit, the downtown Cleveland parade held in honor of the Tribe seemed a bit overdone. Fan favorite Omar Vizquel entertained the crowd with his humor and everyone got to feel good about getting to the Series. There was chatter about what the Indians would do next year, but as one parade goer told the *Cleveland Scene*, "Why are we having a parade for losers?"

"Why are we having a parade for losers?"

THE $2.3 MILLION MAN

Given today's major league baseball salaries, $230,000 a year for 10 years seems like chump change. The New York Yankees had inked Reggie Jackson to a $2.96 million five-year deal on November 29, 1976, but the Cleveland Indians were never in the chase for this costly free agent. However, Tribe general manager Phil Seghi wanted to prove to Tribe fans that the team was serious about signing top talent in order to build a contender. So they targeted a Baltimore Oriole free-agent pitcher named Wayne Garland, who was coming off a 20-9 season in 1976. What should have raised a few eyebrows were Garland's seven wins and ten losses over the previous three seasons. But the Tribe set forth in the uncharted waters of free agency, nonetheless.

Calling the free agent bidding process a "crap shoot," Phil Seghi and team president Ted Bonda landed Garland with a 10-year deal at $230,000 a year. On signing the contract, Garland said, "The money the Indians offered was very good. It was the first and foremost factor in my signing with them." When teased about playing in Cleveland, Garland said he'd play in Siberia for that kind of money. Who could blame him? But for that kind of dough the fans expected their money's worth. The *Sporting News* called the contract "staggering," and the Cleveland media began calling Garland the "2.3 million dollar man." Garland even wore number 23 for a time.

GARLAND SAID HE'D PLAY IN SIBERIA FOR THAT KIND OF MONEY.

In 1977, Garland pitched 283 innings and compiled a 13-19 won-loss record, leading the American League in losses. He had injured himself during his first spring training game in Arizona, and a sore right arm affected his performance all season. He started the 1978 season and went 2-3 when he could battle no longer. The diagnosis was a torn rotator cuff in his pitching shoulder. His 1978 season was over. The Indians had to face the fact that their $2.3 million risk on a pitcher with only one great season was looking ugly. Garland wanted to make good on his contract in the worst way. He came back in 1979 and posted a 4-10 record, followed by a 6-9 record in 1980. He went 3-7 in 1981. On January 29, 1982, the Indians released Garland. But they wouldn't be released from the remaining five years of his contract. These would serve as a painful reminder of Phil Seghi's "crap shoot."

"A torn rotator cuff is a cancer for a pitcher."

—Don Drysdale, Los Angeles

Sports Illustrated Cover Jinx
FROM BEST TO WORST

Sports Illustrated's April 6, 1987, baseball preview edition featured Indians outfielders Corey Snyder and Joe Carter. The headline read, "INDIAN UPRISING. BELIEVE IT. CLEVELAND IS THE BEST TEAM IN THE AMERICAN LEAGUE." The Indians finished 61-101 in last place in the American League East Division.

STANDING TALL

Dino Hall was a diminutive kick returner who played for the Cleveland Browns from 1979–1983. His heart was larger than his 5'-7", 165-pound body, however. After a great performance against the Pittsburgh Steelers, with his parents and family in attendance, reserve linebacker Dave Graf remarked, **"Dino's mom and dad are very proud of him. I bet they feel five feet tall."**

CHAPMAN HIT FRACTURE OF SKULL FEARED

Tragedy

KILLED BY A PITCH

Only once in the history of the major leagues has a player been killed playing the game. That player was Ray Chapman, who wore the uniform of the 1920 Cleveland Indians when felled by a Yankee pitch on Monday, August 16, 1920.

It was the top of the fifth inning at the Polo Grounds on a muggy Monday afternoon in New York. Chapman, or "Chappie" as his teammates called him, led off the fifth, facing Yankee submarine-style pitcher Carl Mays. Mays's fastball sailed in toward Chapman, and the Indians shortstop made no effort to move. Keep in mind that no batting helmets were worn until the Brooklyn Dodgers tried them out in 1941, and helmets weren't mandatory equipment until 1956. The pitch hit Chapman in the left temple, producing a cracking sound heard throughout the ballpark. Several minutes later, Chapman, bleeding from his left ear, was revived and helped to his feet. As he was helped off the field, Chapman's knees buckled, and his mates hoisted his arms around their shoulders for the remainder of the journey. By late Monday, doctors at St. Lawrence Hospital diagnosed a depressed fracture of the skull. In the wee hours of Tuesday morning, doctors attempted to relieve the pressure on Chapman's brain. Vital signs improved after the operation, but the doctors gave no guarantees. At 4:40 a.m. on Tuesday, August 17, 1920, Ray Chapman died.

Jack Graney, Chapman's roommate for several seasons and a future Indians' radio broadcaster, said, "We feel as if we did not care if we ever played baseball again. Perhaps they will play tomorrow. We don't know and we don't care. We cannot imagine ourselves playing with Chapman dead. We did not sleep last night and we cannot eat today. We have lost more than a fellow player. We have lost a real pal." The Indians' players were so outraged at Mays for delivering the killer pitch that they sent a petition to American League president Ban Johnson and the other clubs stating they would never play against Mays again. Johnson and the rest of the American League owners did not lend support to the petition. Mays ended his major league career in 1929 with Hall-of-Fame credentials but was never enshrined at Cooperstown.

As for Ray Chapman's family, his widow, Kathleen, remarried and remained true to her vow never to watch baseball again. She died suddenly in 1928 in what was speculated to be suicide. Ray's mother became a recluse for seven years after attending her son's funeral at Cleveland's St. John Cathedral. The Chapmans' daughter, eight-year-old Rae Marie, died from the measles in 1929, almost a year to the day after her mother's death.

THE 1920 SEASON WAS BITTERSWEET FOR CLEVELAND BASEBALL FANS.

The 1920 season was bittersweet for Cleveland baseball fans. Having endured the tragedy of Chapman's loss, they saw their Indians steady themselves and best the Brooklyn Robins (Dodgers) to win the World Series. Ed Bang of the *Cleveland News* called Chapman the greatest shortstop "ever to wear a Cleveland uniform." While baseball eventually moved beyond this tragedy, Cleveland is forever wedded to this singular event.

TOUGH LUCK

WE MIGHT HAVE HAD MANTLE?

Hugh Alexander had great promise as a ballplayer. The Cleveland Indians signed him to a contract when he finished the 11th grade. Finally, two years later, he played two major league games for the Indians in 1937 and went home to Oklahoma in the off-season to work on the oil rigs. Tragedy struck when young Hugh had his left hand mangled by the gears of the rig on which he was working.

What seemed like the end was just the beginning of a different path. Alexander was offered an Indians scouting job by Cy Slapnicka, the scout who had signed him. In 1938, at the age of 21, he became the youngest scout in major league baseball history. Alexander had to scour the countryside for baseball talent and persuade young players to sign contracts with minor league teams. All totaled, Alexander spent 60 years as a scout, retiring from the Chicago Cubs in 1998. In 1993, the Baseball Writers Association of America named him Scout of the Year. A great story about a legendary baseball scout, right?

Ah, but "Uncle Hughie" had one big regret. In 1948, he was scouting talent in the middle-western states for the Indians and received a tip about a kid from Commerce, Oklahoma. The kid was some kind of athlete, playing both football and baseball, so Alexander paid a visit to the young athlete's high school principal. The school did not have its own baseball team, he learned, so the youngster played in amateur leagues. Also, a football injury had left the kid with a bad leg. "Hell, it's hard enough to make the majors if you're healthy, and when he told me that stuff, I walked out of the school and when I got in my car I took that piece of paper and threw it away. I can still see it blowing across the parking lot," Alexander told author Kevin Kerrane in his book, *Dollar Sign on the Muscle*. The piece of paper had the address of 17-year-old Mickey Mantle written on it. Alexander calls his failure to visit Mantle his "biggest mistake." Indians fans would agree.

ALEXANDER CALLS HIS FAILURE TO VISIT MANTLE HIS "BIGGEST MISTAKE."

When Detroit All-Star outfielder Al Kaline was heckled by a young fan who shouted, "You're not half as good as Mickey Mantle," Kaline replied, "Son, nobody is half as good as Mickey Mantle."

ONLY IN CLEVELAND

A Nice Guy to Arrest

The first draft pick coach Butch Davis ever made for the Cleveland Browns was defensive tackle Gerard Warren from Florida in 2001. Warren was supposed to wreak havoc in the trenches and give the Browns a dominant player for years to come. Gerard was even called "Big Money" because of his huge contract and self-proclaimed big play abilities. One day during the 2002 season, Warren attended a party in Pittsburgh put on by Steelers' wide receiver Plaxico Burress. At 6:23 a.m. on the morning after the party, Warren was stopped by Pittsburgh police in the city's strip and entertainment neighborhood. He was charged with possession of an unregistered, loaded, .45-caliber pistol. The gun was discovered as police were questioning a passenger in Warren's car about suspected drug use. Later, Warren's teammate, tight end O. J. Santiago, was served a warrant for misdemeanor marijuana possession. Warren eventually pled guilty to a misdemeanor firearms charge and was placed on one-year's probation. Needless to say, this incident didn't help the Browns public-relations efforts.

Trying to rescue the bad situation was none other than team president and spin-meister Carmen Policy. He stretched the limit when he confirmed Warren's arrest to the media and added that the Pittsburgh police officer who arrested Warren called him "one of the finest and nicest people he ever arrested." Warren ended up being a non-factor in the Cleveland defense and went to Denver after the 2004 season. As his performance declined, his nickname devalued from "Big Money" to "Penney."

BAD ● TRADE

GOOD INTENTIONS

Halfback Bobby Mitchell teamed up with the great Jim Brown in giving the Browns a versatile running attack in the late 1950s and early 1960s. Often described as the "fleet Bobby Mitchell," the 6-foot, 188-pound sprint champion from the University of Illinois was traded to the Washington Redskins in December 1961 for the Redskins' number one pick in the 1962 NFL draft. The football world was stunned. Bill Scholl of the *Cleveland Press* called it the "biggest deal in their [Browns] history." Everyone knew that the Browns were targeting the talented Syracuse halfback Ernie Davis with the draft pick acquired from Washington. There was competition to sign Davis from the Buffalo Bills of the American Football League, but the Browns banked on winning the signing battle, and they did. Browns head coach Paul Brown felt that Mitchell was an inadequate blocker and couldn't run inside. He wanted a bigger, stronger halfback. Davis was the Syracuse University Heisman trophy winner, who stood 6'-2" and weighed 210 pounds. What could have worked out as one of Cleveland's best deals, however, turned a tragic corner.

Ernie Davis was diagnosed with leukemia and never played a single down for the Browns. Davis passed away in 1963. Mitchell was switched to a flanker-back receiver and became one of the Redskins leading receivers, earning election to the Hall of Fame in 1983. The Browns gambled on the deal, but once signed, Davis was no longer considered a risk. He was going to be Jim Brown's running mate.

Until fate intervened.

1963—JUST ONE BAD THING
AFTER ANOTHER FOR THE BROWNS

The dawning of 1963 saw the city of Cleveland mired in a newspaper strike that silenced its two dailies, the *Cleveland Plain Dealer* and the *Cleveland Press*. One of Cleveland's blockbuster sports stories—the January 9 firing of Paul Brown, the founding head coach of the team that bore his name—could not be covered in the traditional fashion. Hal Lebovitz, sports editor of the *Plain Dealer*, published a booklet, *Paul Brown—The Play He Didn't Call*, which analyzed Brown's sudden axing and featured commentary by other sportswriters. Newspaper-starved Clevelanders consumed nearly 50,000 copies within several days. This wasn't just the firing of a football coach, it was the passing of a legend. *Cleveland Press* sports columnist Frank Gibbons said it best in a column headline: "It was like toppling the Terminal Tower."

THIS WASN'T JUST THE FIRING OF A FOOTBALL COACH.

The new coach, a Paul Brown protégé and assistant, Blanton Collier, was given the job of restoring the team to prominence in the NFL. But first, the team would have to get through the year 1963 and survive a series of events tragic enough to make one wonder: Had team owner Art Modell tempted fate by firing one of the game's most brilliant innovators?

Before he was relieved of his duties, Paul Brown called the shots for the team's 1963 college draft on December 3, 1962. One player the Browns had their eye on was running back Tom Bloom, Purdue University's Most Valuable Player in 1962. Scouts believed Bloom's great athletic ability made him a lock to win a defensive backfield job with the Browns. In the sixth round of the draft, the Browns nabbed him and signed the rookie to a contract that included a signing bonus. But just two days into his new job, Collier had to tell his team that Tom Bloom had been killed in an automobile accident on January 18. Ironically, he was driving the car he had just purchased with his signing bonus money. Tom Bloom never had a chance to bond with his new teammates, yet he would be remembered as a footnote in Browns' history as a member of a tragic triumvirate.

During the fall of 1961, there were glowing reports emanating from Jim Brown's alma mater, Syracuse University, about senior running back Ernie Davis, who had been called "as good or better" than Brown by certain scouts. He had broken many of Brown's Syracuse records and was the first black collegian to win the coveted Heisman Trophy. He endeared himself to others with his genuine nature, prompting one sportswriter to comment that Ernie "was a fourth stringer when talking about himself, but a Heisman winner on the field." Paul Brown wanted Ernie Davis to team-up with Jim Brown in his backfield to provide the one-two punch Green Bay possessed with Jim Taylor and Paul Hornung. The Washington Redskins owned the first pick in the 1962 NFL draft and had designs on Davis. Knowing this, Paul Brown traded Bobby Mitchell, the team's 5'-9", 180-pound star halfback to the Redskins for the first pick, without informing new owner Art Modell.

Davis spent the summer in Chicago practicing with the College All-Stars for their traditional exhibition game against the reigning NFL champions, the Green Bay Packers. After the extraction of bothersome wisdom teeth before the All-Star camp began, Davis experienced swelling around his neck and was hospitalized. On learning of Ernie's hospitalization, Paul Brown told the media, "We're dead if there is anything seriously wrong with Ernie. We're in trouble even if he even misses much practice. We're counting so much on him."

What was first diagnosed as the mumps turned out to be monocytic leukemia. At first doctors kept the diagnosis from Davis, calling it a "blood disorder," but rumors about the shy young halfback's health ran rampant. Davis's treatment brought the disease into remission by late summer, but the most he could do was some light jogging. Once doctors informed him of the true nature of his condition, Davis asked, "Can I lick it?" The answer depended on many factors, the doctors explained, but the obvious was left unspoken. Those close to Davis claimed that he knew his days were numbered.

In an effort to buoy his spirits, the Browns paid a tribute to Davis during the first Pro Football doublehcader at Cleveland Municipal Stadium on August 18, 1962. Having been released from the hospital so he could attend the game, he was introduced for the first and last time to Cleveland fans during the player introductions. Ernie walked onto the darkened stadium field under the glare of a single spotlight. The unassuming athlete from Elmira, New York, was given a thunderous ovation from the 77,000 Browns' faithful. Both the fans and Davis instinctively recognized the poignant truth that Ernie would never play a down for the team that coveted him.

On May 18, 1963, Ernie Davis passed away. In tribute, his Cleveland Browns' Number 45 was retired. Art Modell chartered a plane to transport his mourning coaches and team to Elmira for Davis's funeral. At the end of the service, the Reverend Latta Thomas read the following telegram to those in attendance: "I would like to express my sympathy to you. I had the privilege of meeting Ernie after he had won the Heisman Trophy. He was an outstanding young man of great character who consistently served as an inspiration to the other people of the country." John F. Kennedy, who also had a date with destiny later in 1963, had sent the telegram to Ernie's mother.

HIS CLEVELAND BROWNS' NUMBER 45 WAS RETIRED.

Within three weeks of Davis's death, the Browns were dealt another staggering blow. Their young defensive back, Don Fleming, who had just been named to the All-NFL team by the

CURSES!

"This is perhaps the most morbid sports season in the history of Cleveland."

—The Cleveland Press

Sporting News, was electrocuted in a construction accident in Florida. His untimely death meant the loss of one of the Browns' most popular players and the disruption of the chemistry within the defensive backfield. Once again, Browns' players and coaches made a pilgrimage to mourn a fallen teammate while still grieving another. This time the trip was to Shadyside, Ohio, Fleming's hometown. In paying tribute to Don Fleming, Frank Gibbons of the *Cleveland Press* wrote, "This is perhaps the most morbid sports season in the history of Cleveland. Ernie Davis and now likeable Don Fleming. He can be replaced on the team, but there aren't many athletes like him around."

As the 1963 season began to wind down, the Browns were in championship contention with a 7-3 record and had four games remaining. A home game was on the schedule for November 24, and another bit of tragic irony would play out in this star-crossed season. Coming two days after the assassination of President John F. Kennedy, the Browns would play host to none other than the Dallas Cowboys. In Cleveland, security was doubled at Municipal Stadium over concerns that someone's anger and grief might be exacted on the team representing the city of the president's murder.

When 1963 went in the books, the Browns looked back on a season of tragedy and a second-place finish to the New York Giants. It seemed that the team couldn't catch a break in this mysterious of all seasons, yet cynicism had not yet gained a foothold on the shores of Lake Erie. Cleveland curses were not the sports currency traded in taverns and nightspots. Just as the football gods had taken away in 1963, they would give back a hundredfold the following season.

DUBIOUS DRAFT

GREAT TEAMS ARE BUILT IN THE TRENCHES

In the 1971 NFL draft, the Cleveland Browns selected running back Bo Cornell out of the University of Washington. Still available was offensive tackle Dan Dierdorf from Michigan, who went on to become a five-time All-Pro for the St. Louis Cardinals and was enshrined in the Pro Football Hall of Fame in 1996. Cornell lasted two seasons with the Browns.

NEITHER RAIN NOR SLEET NOR SNOW . . .

While scouting college players for the 1985 NBA Draft, the Cleveland Cavaliers were intrigued by a 6'-9" forward-center who played for Louisiana Tech University. In fact, the Cavaliers were the only team to bring this college junior to Cleveland for two interviews and workout sessions. The consensus around the NBA pegged Louisiana Tech's basketball program a cut below those of upper echelon schools, but the Cavaliers seemed poised to select one of its players with the ninth pick in the first round. The player even told his mother it looked like he was certain Cleveland would take him in the first round. When the time came to make the pick, the Cavaliers' general manager Harry Weltman switched gears and selected Charles Oakley, a native Clevelander from Virginia Union University. Oakley never played for Cleveland. He was traded immediately to the Chicago Bulls in a prearranged deal that enabled the Cavaliers to draft Keith Lee, an All-American from Memphis State University. According to Burt Graeff of the *Cleveland Plain Dealer*, Weltman saw more upside potential in Lee because he played in a big-time college program at Memphis.

CURSES!

What happened to the player from Louisiana Tech in whom the Cavaliers showed so much interest? He was drafted by the Utah Jazz and had a pretty good NBA career, judging by the following statistics:

1. Ranks second in NBA history in points scored (36,374) behind Kareen Abdul-Jabaar (38,387).
2. Was a two-time NBA Most Valuable Player (1996–1997, 1998–1999) and one of only nine NBA players to win the MVP Award more than once.
3. Was a fourteen-time NBA All-Star selection.
4. Holds the NBA all-time record for free throws attempted and free throws made.
5. Ranks second in NBA history in field goals made (13,335) behind Kareem Abdul-Jabaar (15,837).
6. Was selected as one of the "50 Greatest Players in NBA History" in 1996.

Yes, it was Karl Malone. These statistics, plus many more, should have been addressed to the Cleveland basketball fans. But the "Mailman" never made a delivery to the Cavaliers, even though they were ready to stamp him as special delivery with their first pick in 1985.

Tragedy

LITTLE LAKE NELLIE

Halfway through the 1991 baseball season, Mike Hargrove took over as manager of the Cleveland Indians. One day, a new ballpark would be christened and the Tribe would batter opponents with their awesome power. But no one could foresee that on March 22, 1993, nor did it seem important as this awful day came to a close in rural Clermont, Florida.

What began as a precious off day for the Indians ended in tragedy. Indians pitcher Tim Crews invited fellow hurlers Steve Olin and Bob Ojeda to join him at his ranch near Little Lake Nellie in central Florida. The group had originally planned to go fishing in the afternoon, but rain spoiled those plans. Instead, Olin, his wife, and their three small children spent time with Crews's family until the three pitchers boarded the 150-hp-outboard fishing boat for a quick tour around the small lake early in the evening. Dusk began to descend on the lake as Crews gunned the boat's engine and headed off to pick up his friend Perry Brismond. The boat was traveling at a high rate of speed and hit a dock about four feet high, unlighted and invisible to Crews. Brismond recalled hearing the engine rev-up, the sound of a crash, and then an ugly silence. Racing to the point where he last saw the lights of the boat, Brismond discovered the three pitchers in the boat with only Ojeda conscious. Olin had been killed instantly,

THE ANGUISH THAT FOLLOWED WAS, AT TIMES, UNBEARABLE.

and Crews died the next day after emergency surgery failed to save his life. Bob Ojeda survived.

The anguish that followed was, at times, unbearable. A team lost important players but, more importantly, husbands, fathers, and friends were gone forever. Olin's best friend, teammate Kevin Wickander, was devastated over his buddy's death, recalling how he and Olin had drawn straight arrows underneath the bills of their caps to point the way to home plate. This symbol became the rallying point for the Tribe pitchers. Sadly, Bob Ojeda could not answer the question of why he survived while his friends did not. He took a leave from the Indians and hopped a flight to Sweden on the spur of the moment, then returned to the U.S. to check into a psychiatric hospital. He made it back to the Indians in August 1993 but posted the worst numbers of his career. By early 1994, his playing days were through.

Boat crash kills Tribe's Olin

CURSES!

In remembrance of their fallen teammates, the Indians left the jerseys of Olin and Crews hanging in their lockers throughout the season. It has been suggested that Tribe fortunes might have been different if Olin had been the closer throughout the 1990s. For sheer torture, some even imagine Olin winning Game Seven of the 1997 World Series.

In 1995, when the Tribe clinched their first postseason playoff slot in 41 years on a September night in Cleveland, the players celebrated at Jacobs Field by hoisting the Central Division Championship banner. Over the park's sound system came the strains of "The Dance," a song by Garth Brooks. Anyone who had been a Cleveland Indian in 1992 and 1993 knew that was Steve Olin's favorite song. Tribe manager Mike Hargrove requested that it be played that night. He wanted them to remember their fallen teammates, except it would be impossible for them to ever forget.

> *"I still remember walking through that clubhouse door. And the faces said it all. You just couldn't believe it. It made you think you have to enjoy life."*
>
> —Jim Thome, on the day after the Little Lake Nellie tragedy

WHENEVER ...

"He wants to play in Cleveland . . . that's where he wants to end his career next year. And maybe the year after that."

—Baseball broadcaster Bob Uecker on Cleveland Indians pitcher Orel Hershiser's plans for the 1998 season

ONLY IN CLEVELAND

The Pounding on the Mound

Players usually appreciate it when a manager sticks up for them. This was carried to an extreme, however, when Tribe manager Pat Corrales defended Julio Franco in a game against the Oakland Athletics. on July 2, 1986.

During that game, Corrales asked home plate umpire Derryl Cousins if he thought A's pitcher Dave Stewart had thrown intentionally at Tribe hitter Franco. Cousins said he though it was intentional, so Corrales asked that Stewart be ejected. While Cousins and Corrales talked, the scene shifted gears and began to resemble a Bruce Lee movie. Stewart left the pitcher's mound and motioned for Corrales to step toward the mound. "Come on out," Stewart shouted to Corrales. The Tribe skipper accepted the invitation and went out to the mound.

Corrales, a brown-belt in karate, and Stewart, a student of Tae Kwon Do, went at it. Except that Stewart was 29 and Corrales 45 at the time. Corrales fired first with a leg kick to Stewart's rib cage. Stewart easily deflected it. Then Stewart creamed Corrales with a punch to the jaw, and Corrales went down like a sack of cement. The brawl was on, and both benches emptied, with bodies piling on and sucker punches being thrown in the confines of the infield. When the fight was over, 7,379 Kansas City fans shouted, "Replay! Replay!" hoping the fight would be shown on the scoreboard screen, to no avail.

Corrales was unbowed, if a little broken. He said after the game, "The man is 29 years old and I'm 45, but I don't care, I'll still go out there. If I've got to take 60 punches in the face for us to get a win, I'll do it." Stewart simply told reporters, "I meant to break his jaw."

KING GEORGE OF CLEVELAND

Imagine, if you can, the Cleveland Indians as American League champs in 1976, 1977, 1978, 1981, 1996, 1998, 1999, 2000, 2001, and 2003, as well as World Series champions in 1977, 1978, 1996, 1998, 1999, and 2000. While no one will ever know if this really would have happened, a story in Cleveland's past suggests it's a tantalizing might-have-been.

In 1972, the Tribe was owned by local Cleveland frozen-food and restaurant mogul Vernon Stouffer. Stouffer had owned the team since 1967, and he was getting tired of owning it. The team's high point was an 86-75 season in 1968, but in 1971 it skidded to a 60-102 mark. Stouffer began to entertain the idea of sharing the Indians with New Orleans and their new domed stadium. Revenue would be the reason to share the team, but where did the fans figure in? Harrison Dillard of the *Cleveland Press* wrote that this proposal was just "greasing the skids" for eventually moving the team. When the American League owners rejected Stouffer's New Orleans plan, he started thinking about unloading the team.

Behind the scenes, one of Cleveland's prominent businessmen and native sons was watching. According to former *Cleveland Press* sportswriter Bob Sudyk, he had been invited to share drinks with this local entrepreneur at the old Pewter Mug in downtown Cleveland, years before Stouffer's ownership.

"SOMEDAY I'M GONNA OWN THE INDIANS."

When closing time approached and they started to leave, the local man turned to Sudyk and said, "Someday I'm gonna own the Indians." That man was George Steinbrenner.

Fast forward to early 1972. The beleaguered Stouffer needed to unload the Indians for financial reasons. Hank Peters, the Tribe's minor-league director, calls 1970 the year the Cleveland Indians died. It is also well documented that the financial downturn of the Stouffer empire caused Vernon Stouffer's appetite for alcohol to increase. Those doing business with him knew to schedule business meetings before 4:30 p.m. Indians team president Gabe Paul was arranging a deal to link Stouffer with a group willing to negotiate seriously for the Tribe. The deal, if consummated, would relieve Stouffer of the financial drain of owning a major league team, provide Gabe Paul with resources and stability, and satisfy the dream of the syndicate's leader, George Steinbrenner. In a telephone conference involving Vernon Stouffer, his son Jim (a schoolmate of Steinbrenner), Paul, and Steinbrenner's group, the first offer was reportedly $7 million cash for the Indians. Stouffer wanted $8.6 million, and Steinbrenner upped his offer to that figure. Later, Jim Stouffer called to assure Steinbrenner that the deal was done. The jubilant group, which included former Indians great Al Rosen, celebrated.

Exactly what transpired next is not clear. Some reports had Stouffer upset that news of the "deal" had leaked to the Cleveland media. It is known that another group led by then Cleveland Cavaliers' owner Nick Mileti was pursuing Stouffer. In any event, in his next contact with the Steinbrenner group, Vernon Stouffer reportedly mumbled the message that he wasn't interested in the deal at Steinbrenner's price. On March 22, 1972, the Cleveland Indians announced the sale of the team to a weakly financed group headed by Nick Mileti for approximately $10 million.

In his book, *The Curse of Rocky Colavito*, Terry Pluto reports that Herb Score told him there was a handshake deal between Stouffer and Steinbrenner, according to one of Steinbrenner's partners, Steve O'Neil. "He could never figure out why Stouffer backed out, and neither could anyone else," said Score.

Cleveland's loss was Steinbrenner's eventual gain when he and his partners purchased the New York Yankees from the

Columbia Broadcasting System (CBS) for around $10 million in January 1973. The rest is history. Speaking to sportswriter Bob Sudyk for a 1997 *Plain Dealer* article headlined, "The Way Things Might Have Been," Steinbrenner felt he could have resurrected Cleveland baseball fortunes. "No doubt about it. The same strong group of owners that Vernon Stouffer turned down followed me to the Yankees. We had the money and Cleveland then had the biggest ballpark in the country." What about Reggie Jackson? "Reggie? He would have come to Cleveland in a minute. I would have had him thinking Lake Erie was the Riviera."

The Rocky River and Bay Village native still has a soft spot in his heart for Cleveland. In 1972, that heart skipped a beat at the prospect of owning his hometown Indians. It was broken a bit, along with the promises of what might have been, by Vernon Stouffer's clouded reason and lack of vision. As long-time Steinbrenner friend John Minco recalled in a *Cleveland Scene* newspaper story by Michael Roberts, "It is not so much what would have happened with the Indians as what would have happened to the town . . . he would have made a lot of things happen."

> ## *"I'll never have a heart attack.*
> # *I give them."*
> —George Steinbrenner

THE ART OF THE DEAL GONE BAD

One of the Cavaliers' more astute draft picks was their second-round choice in 2002, power forward Carlos Boozer from Duke University. He contributed 10 and 15 points per game in his first two seasons with the Cavaliers. More importantly, he began to mesh well with the Cavs' budding superstar, Lebron James, during the 2003–2004 season. After the season, the Cavaliers' management didn't have to act on Boozer's contract at all. They could pick up his option for 2004–2005 at $695,000 and wait to negotiate a longer-term deal beginning with 2005-2006. But they discussed an alternative with Boozer and his agent in June 2004 in which they would tear up Boozer's $695,000 contract and replace it with a new contract for $5 million. With a wink and a handshake, the Cavs' general manager Jim Paxson thought Boozer would later sign a six-year deal for $40 million. On July 1, 2004, Boozer told the media that he wanted to be in Cleveland because "good things are happening," adding, "it's up to the Cavs and my agent to work things out." Paxson thought he had a salary-cap-friendly side deal in his pocket. But Boozer began seeing other lucrative free-agent deals around the league and had a less than positive meeting with head coach Paul Silas. Because the Cavs foolishly had officially let his option expire, Boozer was free to sign with any NBA team. He inked a six-year, $68 million deal with the Utah Jazz on July 30, 2004. The Cavs could not match this because of salary-cap constraints. It was a crushing blow to the Cavaliers organization, and it made them look inept in NBA circles. Such a side deal was illegal according to the NBA collective bargaining agreement, and the Cavs kept mum about their part in it. Boozer denied ever having a secret handshake deal and said he knew what really happened and "that I'm a man of my word." The Cleveland fans also had a word for Boozer. Confused as to who was responsible for this mess, they began referring to their departed power forward as "Carlos Loozer."

THE CLEVELAND FANS ALSO HAD A WORD FOR BOOZER.

TOUGH LUCK

THE MORE THINGS CHANGE . . .

The line on the January 5, 2003 NFL playoff game between the Browns and Steelers had the Steelers favored by 7½ points. This was supposed to be a contest between a team with legitimate Super Bowl aspirations and a team just happy to be in the playoffs. No doubt, the first playoff appearance in the "new Browns" era made every Cleveland fan happy, but that happiness turned to elation as the Browns owned a 17-point lead in the third quarter. Visions of beating the Steelers began to take shape as the game went on. The Cleveland offense was led by backup quarterback Kelly Holcomb, and he had the offense firing on all cylinders. He shredded the Pittsburgh defense for 429 yards passing. Pittsburgh, on the other hand, was killing itself with turnovers—two interceptions and a fumble early in the contest. But the Browns could only manage seven points out of three turnovers, otherwise they might have demoralized the Steelers early.

Throughout the game and during crunch time in the fourth quarter, the Browns' inability to grind it out on the ground hurt them badly. Holcomb was forced to throw on nearly every play, and the Steelers knew it. Still, with 10 minutes remaining in the game, the Browns were on top 33-21. Even Steelers' fans were finding their way out of Heinz Field thinking the game could not be salvaged. A few of the Steelers' players were congratulating their opponents on an amazing game. But Steelers quarterback Tommy Maddox suddenly awakened and led a 77-yard scoring drive that ate chunks off the clock. Browns 33—Steelers 28. What did the Browns need? A first down, maybe two, in order to put the Steelers away. But with no running game, the Browns quickly faced a third down and 12 yards to go. A Holcomb pass to Dennis Northcutt was dropped. "I just dropped it, plain and simple. It hurt standing on the sideline know-

BITTER END FOR BROWNS

ing I could have secured the game," lamented the receiver who had two scores and a long punt return.

After a Browns punt, Maddox took over again a drove his team halfway down the field for a score with 54 seconds left. The Steelers were successful on the two-point conversion to make the margin three points. A field goal could tie, but with the Browns limited to the pass, the Steelers had them right where they wanted them. It ended bitterly for Browns fans, once again, losing to the Steelers by a score of 36-33. As the *Plain Dealer's* Bud Shaw wrote the morning after, "They are the old Browns now. This was the christening. And even more certainly, they understand their place in the undeniable tradition of playoff collapses."

BLACK CATS AND RABBITS' FEET

Every now and then in major league baseball, a single pitcher or hitter ends up "owning" another team. Whether the player is simply lucky or finds and exploits their weaknesses is immaterial. In baseball, superstition reigns supreme as teams try to snap losing streaks and break jinxes. Nowhere was this more evident than in the saga of the Cleveland Indians vs. Eddie Lopat, a pitcher for the Chicago White Sox (1944–1947), New York Yankees (1948–1955), and Baltimore Orioles (1955). Lopat dominated the Cleveland Indians with a career record of 40 wins and 12 losses, a staggering .769 winning percentage. Did Lopat intimidate Tribe batters with blazing speed and brush-back pitches? Was he brash and cocky? Quite the contrary, Lopat was called the "Junkman" because he threw slow, looping pitches that kept hitters off balance and frustrated. When he really needed it, "Steady Eddie" would reach back and fire a fastball right past a hitter who had been hypnotized by his off-speed pitches.

In 1954, when the Tribe won 111 games and a trip to the World Series, Lopat had no trouble beating them five times. Searching for a way to break the curse, the Indians' management began selling rabbits' feet on the days Lopat pitched in Cleveland. Still, the jinx continued. Lopat used to chuckle over the time the Indians tried to beat him at his own game. He recalled a 1949 game in Cleveland when he and a few teammates arrived at Municipal Stadium to escape the sweltering heat of their hotel. They arrived in mid-afternoon for an 8 p.m. game and noticed the Tribe players taking batting practice nearly two hours ahead of schedule. Throwing batting practice was left-handed pitcher Sam Zoldak, imitating Lopat's junk pitches. When Yankee catcher Yogi Berra showed up at the ballpark, Lopat told him not to call for any junk pitches—just fastballs and sliders. The first time through the lineup, the Indians were geared to hit his junk. Lopat then switched to the junk and the frustrated Tribe went down to defeat, 5-3.

In another outing in Cleveland, as Eddie walked to the mound at Municipal Stadium for the first inning, a loyal Tribe fan ran onto the field and hurled a black cat at him. Catching the frightened cat, Lopat handed it to an usher for safekeeping, and then slow-pitched his way to another victory over the Indians. For whatever reason, Eddie Lopat had the Indians' number. No, he didn't stop them from becoming world champs in 1948. But had they faced him just one more time, it might have been the Boston Red Sox representing the American League in the World Series. Cleveland fans would have been forever haunted by the "Curse of Eddie Lopat."

DUBIOUS DRAFT

KICKING OURSELVES

In the 1973 NFL draft, the Cleveland Browns selected wide receiver Steve Holden out of Arizona State University. Still available was punter Ray Guy from Southern Mississippi University. Guy is considered one of the greatest punters in the history of the NFL, with a 14-year career spent with the Oakland Raiders. He made the Pro Bowl seven times. In 1994 he was the only punter selected to the NFL's 75th Anniversary Team. Holden lasted with the Browns until 1976 and played the 1977 season with Cincinnati before leaving football.

BIG HOUSE ON THE PRAIRIE

The story of the Richfield Coliseum is also a big part of the Nick Mileti story. Mileti, Cleveland native son and sports promoter, envisioned a sports and entertainment complex as a catalyst for merging the metropolitan areas of Cleveland and Akron. An interesting idea, but after only 25 years the house that Nick built fell to the wrecking ball in 1999.

It was on October 26, 1974, that Mileti hosted the gala opening of his $25 million palace by presenting Frank Sinatra in concert. "Old Blue Eyes" cost Mileti $250,000, and those attending had trouble getting to the Coliseum because all the parking areas weren't yet completed. Many Sinatra lovers parked their cars on the shoulders of Interstate 271 and Route 303 and walked up embankments, decked in their tuxedos and evening gowns.

The next week, the first sporting event, a Cleveland Crusaders hockey game, was cancelled because the ice-making equipment wouldn't cooperate. But over the years, the Coliseum operations improved and helped increase attendance for Mileti's basketball Cavaliers, the hockey Crusaders, World Team Tennis, and other entertainment events. In the excitement of the 1976 Cavaliers' "Miracle of Richfield" season, the crowds that packed the house rocked the building till the roof shook. The facility was one of the first to have private suites, a restaurant with a view of the game or entertainment event, and a video scoreboard. But, alas, the building's location at the junction of Interstate 271 and Ohio Route 303 proved to be its undoing. The much-hoped-for convergence of Cleveland and Akron and the accompanying real estate development boom never occurred. Cleveland fans eventually tired of the trip "out to the Coliseum," and there wasn't much nightlife in the area for post-event gatherings. Cleveland's Gund brothers, Gordon and George, took ownership of the Coliseum in 1981 and vacated the premises when they moved the Cavaliers to the new downtown Gund Arena in 1994. By 1999 they concluded the sale of the land to the Trust for Public Land

THE BUILDING'S LOCATION PROVED TO BE ITS UNDOING.

for $9.27 million. The trust later sold it to the Cuyahoga Valley National Recreation Area. There was developer interest in the site, including rumors of turning it into a prison, but the Gunds wanted the land to be returned to the public park authority. The Coliseum was demolished and buried in the earth from which it once rose. With it went the dream of a renaissance that never really bloomed.

Sports Illustrated Cover Jinx

THE WIZARD CAN'T BREAK THE SPELL

A week prior to the 1986 AFC Championship game against Denver, the Browns had beaten the Jets in double overtime. Ozzie Newsome was featured on the cover of *Sports Illustrated* after the thrilling victory. When asked about the vaunted "SI jinx," Ozzie said, "This is our year for cracking jinxes. We won in Pittsburgh and we won a playoff game." Right.

ONLY IN CLEVELAND

The Looniest Trade

It was done only once in the history of major league baseball and, yes, it had Indians general manager Frank Lane's fingerprints all over it. On August 3, 1960, Lane pulled the trigger on what many consider to be his looniest trade. He sent his manager, Joe Gordon, to Detroit for Tigers' manager Jimmie Dykes, topping off a trifecta of notorious trades in the 1960 season. On April 17, 1960, Lane and the Tigers' general manager, William DeWitt, were partners in the Rocky-Colavito-for-Harvey-Kuenn trade. One day later Lane traded another Tribe favorite, left-handed pitcher Herb Score, to the Chicago White Sox for pitcher Barry Latman. Now, this major league manager swap.

There was plenty of speculation as to why. Frank Lane portrayed Bill DeWitt as the instigator. While the two GMs were talking about other deals, Lane recalled DeWitt saying, "Let's make a big one. It's something that's never been tried before. Let's change managers." Lane said he then took the idea to Gordon, who was surprisingly agreeable. The *Cleveland Plain Dealer* presented a different slant on the trade, saying that certain Tribe players believed the trade resolved a rift between outfielder Jimmy Piersall and Joe Gordon.

Whatever the real reason, in 1959 the Tribe couldn't overtake the Chicago White Sox for the American League pennant and finished five games behind them. Lane publicly criticized Gordon's managing of the club down the stretch. To Lane's secret delight, Gordon announced his resignation with seven games to play. Lane attempted to hire Leo Durocher as the Tribe's new manager, but Durocher's asking price and the popularity of Gordon forced Lane into hiring him back. Lane finally got the chance to unload Gordon 96 games into the 1960 season when the Tiger's DeWitt "suggested" the trade.

At the time of the trade, the Tribe was sitting in fourth place at

50-46 and had lost 9 of 12 games. Jimmie Dykes' comment on the deal was not very comforting for Tribe fans. "I'm bringing no magic to Cleveland. If I had any, I would have used it on the Tigers." That's for sure. The Indians finished in fourth place, 21 games behind the New York Yankees, while Gordon piloted the Tigers to a sixth place finish, 26 games behind the Yanks. Exactly two months to the day he was traded to Detroit, Joe Gordon resigned as manager of the Tigers, citing interference from team president Bill DeWitt, the man who traded for him. Dykes concluded his managerial career with Cleveland in 1961.

"It looks like about the most ridiculous, outlandish, amateurish, and nonsensical [trade] anybody could think up—and if we could think of anything else sarcastic to say about it we would."

—*Cleveland Press* editorial, August 3, 1960

TOO LITTLE, TOO LATE, TOO EXPENSIVE

His consistent hitting and skilled defense made Keith Hernandez one of the better first basemen to play the game of baseball. Hernandez was a National League player from 1974 to 1989 where he toiled for the St. Louis Cardinals and the New York Mets. He was the National League's Most Valuable Player in 1979 and won 11 straight Gold Gloves. He left the Mets as a free agent in November 1989 and signed a two-year deal worth about $3.5 million with the Cleveland Indians a month later. Knowing they were picking him up at the end of the line, Cleveland wound up overpaying for a whopping 43 games and 130 at-bats from Keith in 1990.

JIM BROWN RETIRES

The greatest running back of all time rushed into the record books right here in Cleveland. It didn't get much better than Jim Brown playing for the Cleveland Browns from 1957 through 1965. He was the NFL's Rookie of the Year in 1957, made nine Pro Bowls in nine years, and was one of the most durable players the league has ever seen. His 12,312 rushing yards and combined 15,459 yards placed him in a class by himself for many years. After Brown helped Cleveland win the NFL Championship in 1964 and just miss winning it in 1965, fans looked forward to the potential for more championships. But in the summer of 1966, Jim Brown stunned the entire sports world by announcing his retirement at the age of 30. He made his announcement from London, England, where he was filming the movie *The Dirty Dozen*. Brown stated, "I am no longer mentally prepared to play. My mind is on other things."

Brown Leaves Pro Football at Top of Career

Tragedy

A SENSELESS LOSS

The Browns finally hit big in the NFL draft of 1984. They selected safety Don Rogers from UCLA with their first-round pick. Rogers was a big hitter and made huge strides in claiming a leadership role on the team's defense. He was named the AFC Defensive Rookie of the Year in 1984 and was poised for a breakout year in 1986. On the eve of his wedding in June 1986, Rogers died of a cocaine overdose. Investigations did not substantiate any link to Rogers's bachelor party held the night before his death. Several Browns' teammates were in attendance and described the party as "tame and uneventful." The mystery concerning Rogers's drug habits was disconcerting for friends, family, and the Browns' organization. A talented future All-Pro safety was lost, senselessly.

HE SAVED THE BEST FOR LAST

The fans of Cleveland laughed when Browns owner Art Modell hired Bill Belichick as the team's new head coach in 1991, especially when he vowed, **"If I'm wrong about this man, I should consider getting out of football."** It was typical Modell bombast, and many fans hoped he would make good on his promise if Belichick failed. In Belichick's five seasons as head coach (1991–1995), he led the team to a .493 winning percentage, one of the worst in Browns' history. The last laugh was on the poor fans. The Browns moved, and Belichick went on to "Super" fame as he coached the New England Patriots to three Super Bowl championships.

BIGGEST BUMMERS
THE FUMBLE

This one's painful.

It was January 17, 1988, and Cleveland Browns' football fans had been given the green light by their doctors to watch the 1987 AFC Championship game. Most of the previous year had been spent healing broken hearts, minds, and spirits as a result of the trauma inflicted by John Elway in the 1986 AFC title game. Beating Denver would definitely wipe away the post-traumatic stress of "The Drive" and put the Browns in the Super Bowl, where they should have gone a year earlier. Yes, this was revenge!

It looked as if this game might be over before halftime as the Browns found themselves down 14-0 at the end of the first quarter and 21-3 at the half. Quarterback Bernie Kosar was intercepted early in the game, which set the stage for the first of three John Elway touchdown passes in the first half. But in the second half, the Browns fought their way back, slicing the lead to 21-10 on a Kosar-to-Reggie Langhorne TD pass. Elway, not to be outdone, drove his team to reestablish an 18-point lead at 28-10. Two Cleveland touchdowns, a 32-yard Kosar-to-Earnest Byner TD pass, and a four-yard Byner TD run had the Browns in the thick of it, trailing only 28-24. Right before the third quarter ended, a Denver field goal put the Broncos up 31-24, but the Browns answered early in the fourth quarter to tie it at 31-31.

Despite the valiant Browns' effort, Cleveland fans knew better than to count on a victory. The Mile High Stadium crowd was into this game, just as the Dawg Pound had tried to make life difficult for the Broncos a year before. And every Browns' fan knew never to count John Elway out. Their fears seemed to be confirmed as Elway's touchdown pass to Sammy Winder at 4:01 to play gave the Broncos a 38-31 lead. Then, as Kosar moved his team to the Denver eight-yard line with 1:05 left in the game, hopes were lifted. The next play, known as "Trap 13," was a handoff to running back Earnest Byner. Byner had played a spectacular game so far. He had rushed for 67 yards, had 120 yards receiving, and had scored two touchdowns. Byner headed toward the left side of the Browns' line and appeared destined for the end zone and the game-tying score. Could we win in regulation, with so little time left? Or would we simply take our chances in overtime? These were questions answered abruptly by Denver defensive back Jeremiah Castille, who sealed Byner's opening to the goal line, stripped him of the ball, and then recovered it for Denver. This time there would be no overtime, only another name to add to the sports lexicon of Cleveland.

"The Fumble" would become the evil-twin of "The Drive."

"As an individual, I probably played the best game of my life that day. Unfortunately, the one play stands out and it should. At that particular time, I felt I had let everybody down."

—Earnest Byner

ONLY IN CLEVELAND

Foggy Logic

Early in the baseball season, games played at Cleveland Municipal Stadium on the lakefront could be quite unpredictable because of the fickle weather. On May 26, 1986, a night contest between the Boston Red Sox and the Indians was delayed twice because of intense fog that rolled in off the lake. Umpires requested that practice fly balls be hit to the outfielders to determine visibility before they decided to resume play. Finally, the game was called in the bottom of the sixth inning, with Boston winning 2-0. After the game, which was referred to as the "Fog Game," Boston pitcher Dennis "Oil Can" Boyd remarked, "That's what they get for building a stadium next to the ocean."

DUBIOUS DRAFT

DINNER BELL MEL

There was no doubt that the Cleveland Cavaliers were looking for a big center to plug the middle on draft day in 1984. The Cavs took Tim McCormick, a 6'-11" Michigan center, with their first pick amidst the boos of fans at their annual draft-day party. After the Washington Bullets drafted 7', 246-pound Kentucky center Mel Turpin, the Cavs traded McCormick and veteran Cliff Robinson for him, and the fans were beside themselves with glee. They figured the Cavs now had the dominating center any successful team must have, plus, he had the college nickname of "Big Dipper." Turpin had also earned recognition with the Kentucky Wildcats as one of the "Twin Towers" along with 7'-1" Sam Bowie, and he seemed like a great choice.

But wait—there were some early warning signals. Turpin had turned down a tryout with the U.S. Olympic team saying he was out of shape. Then, *Plain Dealer* columnist Hal Lebovitz wrote that if Turpin showed some heart and was aggressive, the pick would be a good one. Lebovitz felt Turpin hadn't shown much in the NCAA finals against Georgetown and Patrick Ewing. Still, nicknames like the "Big Dipper" and "Twin Towers" were enticing.

Turpin played three seasons with the Cavaliers, was traded to the Utah Jazz on October 8, 1987, and was out of the NBA after two more. His nickname by 1987 had changed to "Dinner Bell" Mel. It was said that the only thing Mel could post up was the room service menu in his hotel room. Lebovitz was proved right: Turpin only showed hunger at the dinner table, not on the court.

THERE WERE SOME EARLY WARNING SIGNALS

CURSES!

SHOULD'VE KEPT ECK

In the 1972 amateur draft, the Indians selected a gung-ho shortstop from Niagara Falls, New York, and a hard-throwing pitcher from Fremont, California. Both played together in the minor leagues and became close friends. At 17 years of age, both players possessed the confidence and ability to make it to the big leagues. By the start of the 1975 season, Indians manager Frank Robinson had the young pitcher wearing a Cleveland uniform. By June, the former high school shortstop was patrolling the expanses in center field at Municipal Stadium. Dennis Eckersley and Rick Manning were back together again—inseparable.

In 1977, Eckersley was rounding into a phenomenal pitcher, posting 22⅓ hitless innings over three games, falling two thirds of an inning shy of tying Cy Young's 1904 record of 23 hitless innings. Manning was playing with reckless abandon. But with a headfirst slide on the Astroturf at the Seattle Kingdome on June 4, 1977, he fractured his back and sat out for most of the year and finished with a weak .226 batting average.

What happened next falls squarely in the category of "only in Cleveland." The Indians made an error in the contract they sent to Manning for the 1978 season, technically making Manning a free agent. The Indians did not want to be exposed for their blunder, so they negotiated a five-year $2.5 million contract to keep Manning, banking that he would return to star status. Cleveland fans were more than a bit troubled over awarding millions to a player with a broken back.

THE INDIANS DID NOT WANT TO BE EXPOSED FOR THEIR BLUNDER.

But they were even more stunned when, on March 30, 1978, their fire-balling right-hander was traded to the Boston Red Sox along with catcher Fred Kendall in exchange for catcher Bo Diaz, infielder Ted Cox, and pitchers Mike Wise and Mike Paxton. It was shades of the 1960 Rocky Colavito trade—a young, gifted player with whom Cleveland could identify, senselessly dealt away. Senseless, that is, unless you were the Indians front office, who knew that Rick Manning was having an affair Eckersley's wife, a situation that could only turn ugly for the best friends and teammates.

The Indians spun a story that they were concerned about Dennis's sidearm motion wearing down his arm and shortening his career, but they knew they had to split up the duo before the awkward personal situation had the whole team picking sides. Tribe management traded Eckersley because Manning, coming off his back injury, was damaged goods and would not garner much in the trade market. Besides, the Tribe front office thought Manning would end up being the better player in the long run.

Guess again. Eckersley played 24 years, was selected an All-Star six times, and was enshrined in the Hall of Fame in 2004. Manning played 13 years, was never named an All-Star, and finished his career with the Milwaukee Brewers.

········· **ONLY IN CLEVELAND** ·········

Fashion Victims

One of the benefits of owning a major league baseball team is that you can do pretty much whatever you want with your team. From 1972–1975, Jim Stouffer, son of Indians owner Vernon Stouffer, dressed his players in "fire-injun red" jerseys and pants for their home games. The Indians looked like a company softball team, and the players were so embarrassed that they paid to have more sedate blue jerseys and white pants. First baseman Boog Powell dubbed himself the "world's biggest Bloody Mary" when he donned the all-red uniform.

STEPIEN STRIKES AGAIN

When Bill Laimbeer finished his NBA career in 1993, he was the all-time leader in rebounds for his team, averaged 12.9 points per game, and had his number retired. Too bad it wasn't for the team that drafted him in 1979. The Cavaliers took him in the third round of the 1979 NBA draft but didn't get around to offering the Notre Dame lad a contract until August of that year. By then, Laimbeer had made the decision to play in Italy and didn't return to play for Cleveland until the 1980–1981 season. He averaged 30 minutes and 9.8 minutes per game, with 693 total rebounds in his first season, but was traded to the Detroit Pistons in February 1982 along with forward Kenny Carr for Phil Hubbard, Paul Mokeski, and two additional draft picks. The Ted Stepien–led Cavaliers brainless trust blundered by sending Laimbeer to the Pistons before giving him a chance to develop. Gaining a reputation as an on-the-court villain and enforcer, Laimbeer became a four-time All-Star and the nineteenth player in NBA history to rack up 10,000 points and 10,000 rebounds in a career. He and the rest of the Piston "Bad Boys" won the NBA crown in 1989 and 1990. He fought the injury bug but owns the longest consecutive game streak in the NBA at 685 games. Never afraid to throw an elbow or intimidate on the court, it is said he was punched by the NBA's finest, including Bob Lanier, Robert Parish, Charles Barkley, and Larry Bird. The Cavs could have used a bit of Laimbeer's spirit, had they not been so short sighted.

THE CAVS COULD HAVE USED A BIT OF LAIMBEER'S SPIRIT

Tragedy

DEATH FROM ABOVE

The Cleveland National Air Races were conceived in 1929 by a group of Cleveland-area businessmen led by Louis W. Greve and Frederick C. Crawford. Greve was president of Cleveland Pneumatic Tool Company, and Crawford was the eventual president of Thompson Products, now part of TRW, Inc. The event evolved into a gigantic 10-day affair with spectators coming from all over the country to see Goodyear blimps, parachute jumping, and sky-walking. The main attraction was an event called close-course racing that was five laps around a pylon-lined 10-mile course. It was a real free-for-all as flyers competed for the coveted Thompson Trophy. In 1929, pilot Thomas Reid crashed in Fairview Park near Hopkins Airport as he tried to set an endurance flying record. As tragic as the accident was, it was a possibility accepted by all pilots who engaged in this type of competition.

After World War II, the races resumed, and there were more advanced aircraft as a result of the war's technology. The pilot to beat in 1949 was a former Thompson Products employee, Cook Cleland. Another racer, Bill Odom, was closing in on Cleland over the city of Berea when he cut too sharply around a pylon, flipped upside-down, and crashed into a home, killing a mother and her young son. This marked the first time anyone other than pilots had been killed in an air show. The U.S. Government Defense Department immediately cut all military assistance to the show, and it ceased operations. The shows resumed in Cleveland in 1964 at the Burke Lakefront Airport with Formula 1 racing introduced in 1967.

CURSES!

DUBIOUS DRAFT

OVERLOOKED IN OUR OWN BACKYARD

In the 1974 NFL draft, the Cleveland Browns selected offensive line-man Bill Corbett from little Johnson C. Smith College in the second round. Still on the draft board was Kent State University linebacker Jack Lambert. Lambert is well known to Cleveland Browns fans be-cause he made life miserable for Cleveland quarterbacks for 11 years as a member of the Pittsburgh Steelers. He made nine consecutive Pro Bowls and was enshrined in the Football Hall of Fame in 1990. The accolades go on and on. Suffice it to say that Lambert is often referred to as the best middle linebacker to play the game of foot-ball. Corbett did not make Cleveland's 1974 team and never played professional football.

BAD TRADE

A FIVE-TOOL PLAYER

In baseball, "five-tool player" is a term describing an athlete who hits for an average, hits for power (home runs and runs-batted in), pos-sesses speed and a good throwing arm, and can play great defense. On December 11, 2001, the Cleveland Indians were convinced they had acquired such a player in outfielder Alex Escobar. Baseball America rated him the 18th best prospect in their spring 2001 ratings.

THERE WAS A CATCH TO SECURING THIS POTENTIAL STAR, HOWEVER.

There was a catch to securing this potential star, however. The Indians had to trade future Hall of Fame second baseman Robbie Alomar to the New York Mets in a multi-player deal that had Cleveland fans hopping mad. Suddenly, Escobar became the most important player in the Indians organization because of the price they paid for him. In his first big deal as the new general manager of the Indians, Mark Shapiro knew this deal would be unpopular. He told the media that the club needed "to get a little younger" and take a step backward to eventually take a big step forward. "He's not ready to put it all together now," Shapiro said of Escobar, "so there's an obvious risk factor. But the fact is, he's still a five-tool player."

But the step backward was a disastrous one as Escobar went into the outfield wall during a 2002 spring training game and tore up his left knee. After reconstructive knee surgery, he returned to the Tribe's minor leagues in 2003 and eventually played 28 games for the Indians. In 2004, Escobar struggled early in the big league season with a .211 batting average, 12 runs-batted in and 1 home run in 152 at-bats. Sent to the minors again, he suffered another setback in his quest to gain a spot with the Indians when he broke the navicular bone in his right foot. The Tribe finally cut their ties with Escobar in July. On August 16, 2004 he was picked up by the Chicago White Sox who traded him to the Washington Nationals in February 2005. His arm strength and defense is still considered to be in the top tier of American League outfielders, but the oft-injured Escobar seems to have lost three of his five tools to a string of injuries. He may only be remembered as the player received for Robbie Alomar.

ONLY IN CLEVELAND

Go West, Young Man

Indians outfielder and pinch-hitter "Sweet Lou" Johnson paid a visit to a local Cleveland Cadillac dealer on the last day of the 1968 season. Apparently his smooth style and charm helped him talk the salesman into giving him a test drive of a Coup de Ville. Lou "tested" it all the way to his home in Los Angeles.

TOUGH LUCK

THE WORST RUG BURN EVER

The Cleveland Browns' 1970 college draft will always be remembered as the time Paul Warfield was traded for the first-round draft rights to Purdue quarterback Mike Phipps. While this move turned sour for the Browns, they struck gold in the second round. Oklahoma State had yielded one of those rare combinations of toughness, smarts, and athletic ability in a 6'-4", 250-pound body belonging to Jerry Sherk. Jerry progressed from a scrub on his high school team in Grants Pass, Oregon, to a collegiate wrestler and tenacious defensive tackle for the Oklahoma State Cowboys. Jerry tells the story of flying to Cleveland in 1970 with his "spirits 10,000 feet higher than the 727" he was sitting in. "The only thing that was important," he recalls, "was that I was going to be a Cleveland Brown."

He was much more, having been named to the Pro Bowl in four consecutive seasons (1974–1977), and was selected the NFL's best defensive lineman in 1975. He notched 69 career quarterback sacks and had four in one game in 1976. In 1979, Sherk had 12 sacks over the course of 11 games. Not bad for someone who, when he made his pro debut in the first-ever Monday Night Football game in 1970, was roundly criticized by commentator Howard Cosell.

Sadly, Sherk's career ended way too soon. Compared to what might have happened to him, being forced to quit pro football pales in comparison. Still referred to as the Browns' greatest defensive lineman, Jerry nearly lost his life due to complications from a staph infection. On November 4, 1979, the Browns traveled to Philadelphia, where they defeated the Eagles in what Sherk describes as an "unremarkable game, except that I recall that I had received a terrible rug burn on my right arm due to the [artificial] turf." The resulting infection settled in Sherk's most vulnerable spot—his surgically repaired left knee. Complications and a long hospital stay cost him about 40 pounds and sapped his strength. "After the operation," said Sherk, "they were scared that the infection hadn't been arrested as I still had a high fever. They had talked about taking my leg if the infection became active again. Luckily, my fever was due to an antibiotic that I was allergic to."

Sherk was determined to make it back. Sacrificing the 1980 season to rest and rehabilitation, the Browns' defensive stalwart remembers, "I tried one more year in 1981 but was ineffective as a pass rush specialist. It was then I decided to retire, before the coaches looked at the film and decided to retire me." The fight for his life had robbed

SHERK WAS DETERMINED TO MAKE IT BACK.

Jerry of speed and quickness—his two most valuable assets. Cleveland would not see him stuff the opponents' offense in what could have been a 1980 Super Bowl season, nor would they again take pride in pointing to Number 72 as their perennial All-Pro, even in dismal seasons. Sadly, the pending reservation for a trip to Canton, Ohio was canceled not by choice, but circumstance.

Among peers and coaches, Sherk was considered one of the most dominating defensive players of his era. Jerry's first coach with the Browns, Blanton Collier, maintained that "Absolutely nobody was better than Jerry Sherk." Sherk's early departure from the NFL is truly one of Cleveland's bad breaks.

LIP SERVICE

HOT ROD'S HEAT

In August 1990, the NBA's Miami Heat signed Cleveland Cavaliers' restricted free agent John "Hot Rod" Williams to an offer sheet. Although the Cavs eventually matched the offer to retain Williams, he told the media, **"Well, right now, I guess I'm a Heat."**

THE CHAMPIONSHIP OF OUR DREAMS

It didn't get nominated for an Oscar, but it's ours, and we love it. Written and directed by David Ward, the 1989 movie *Major League* is about a former showgirl who marries the owner of the Cleveland Indians. The owner doesn't survive the honeymoon, and she owns the club. The way out to a warmer climate and a bigger stadium is to have poor attendance in Cleveland, so she tries to field the worst team she can find. When the misfits on the team discover that their new owner is doing all she can to make the team lose, the players get fired-up and begin to win, and attendance picks up. The Tribe ends up in a one-game play-off with the New York Yankees, which it wins in dramatic fashion. Of course, beat-up veteran Cleveland catcher Jake Taylor (played by Tom Berenger) gets the girl (Rene Russo) in the end. The story line contains the old junkball pitcher, Eddie Harris (Chelcie Ross); the big, strong player who cannot hit a curve ball to save his life, Pedro Cerrano (Dennis Haysbert); the conceited endorsement-hungry pretty-boy, Roger Dorn (Corbin Bernsen); and the ex-con pitcher, Rick "Wild Thing" Vaughn (Charlie Sheen).

It is well known that though the movie takes place in Cleveland, the stadium scenes were filmed at Milwaukee County Stadium. What did you expect from a movie about Cleveland? When the stadium scoreboard is shown, a sign for Milwaukee radio station WTMJ is in view. Ex-major leaguer and broadcaster Bob Uecker plays Tribe play-by-play man Harry Doyle. Uecker is from Milwaukee, and the rumor was that he wouldn't appear in the film if it wasn't filmed in Milwaukee. But there are some outside shots of Cleveland Municipal Stadium as well as an overhead view filmed from a helicopter on the night of a real Indians game in Cleveland, when from the announcer's booth,

Harry Doyle says, "In case you haven't noticed, and judging by the attendance you haven't, the Indians have managed to win a few ball games and are threatening to climb out of the cellar." SportsCritics.com has developed its "100 Greatest Sports Movie Quotes" and *Major League* contributes seven of them:

98. "How's your wife and my kids?" Catcher Jake Taylor to Yankees hitter Clue Haywood.

68. Willie Mays Hayes (Wesley Snipes): "I hit like Mays and I run like Hayes."

     Manager Lou Brown (James Gammon): "You may run like Hayes but you hit like sh—."

51. Manager Lou Brown to Rick "Wild Thing" Vaughn in the playoff game with the Yankees: "Forget the curve ball Rickey, give him the heater."

47. Eddie Harris to Pedro Cerrano: "You trying to say Jesus Christ can't hit a curveball?"

36. Eddie Harris, when drinking Pedro Cerrano's rum and talking to Cerrano's voo-doo idol: "Up your butt, Jobu!"

32. An Indians' pitch is several yards outside the strike zone and Harry Doyle exclaims, "Juuuust a bit outside."

18. Ricky Vaughn's reply to where he played before coming to the Indians: "California Penal."

"Tuesday is Die Hard Night. Free admission for anyone who was actually alive the last time the Indians won a pennant."

—Indians radio announcer Harry Doyle, played by Bob Uecker, in the movie, *Major League*

CURSES!

ONLY IN CLEVELAND

Zeus Erupts

It could have happened anytime, anywhere, to any player, but the chances of it actually happening seemed slim. On December 19, 1999, NFL referee Jeff Triplette made dubious history as he tossed a yellow penalty flag toward the Browns' offensive line as they lined up for a second quarter play against the Jacksonville Jaguars. The yellow penalty flag is supposed to be tossed up in the air, but Triplette's toss had more of a Randy Johnson fastball velocity on it. It flew through the facemask of an innocent lineman's helmet, striking him in the right eye. The yellow flag is supposed to help protect players from illegal actions that could bring injury. This time, the penalty flag brought injury, pain, and ultimate embarrassment to a player and his team.

The player was Browns' offensive lineman Orlando Brown, nick-named "Zeus." His size and a terrifying temper that resembled thunderbolts from Mount Olympus made the nickname apropos. Now, with his right eye swollen shut from the impact of the BB-weighted flag, Brown took refuge on the sideline while holding the right side of his helmet in obvious pain, but he quickly returned to the field. Browns head coach Chris Palmer said he thought Brown was courageously going back to rejoin his teammates in the huddle. But Zeus, who boasted one time that he was the "top dirtiest player in the league," was not thinking clearly, if he was thinking at all. Brown delivered an unprecedented two-handed shove to Jeff Triplette's chest that sent the official hurtling to the ground, shocking both the Browns and Jaguars players. The 350-pound Brown loomed over the fallen 195-pound Triplette, and both teams had to hold him back to prevent further assault. Brown was ejected from the game and escorted to the sideline, where he suffered another meltdown, kicking the yardage chains and engaging in a shouting match with his head coach.

When things settled down, the revelations were many. Brown was seriously injured, suffering vision impairment and bleeding within the eye socket. He also was the first player in NFL history to be suspended for more than one game for physical contact with an official. While in the hospital, Brown revealed that his violent outburst was due to his fear of vision loss since his father's glaucoma-induced sight loss in 1993. But Brown's temper had a history, as the *Plain Dealer's* Bud Shaw wrote the day after the incident. Referring to Brown's playing days with the "old" Browns under Bill Belichick, it seemed that Belichick "used to call Brown into his office before games and stoke him with threats until Brown left the office raging like a five-alarm fire."

While the NFL expressed concern for Brown's health, Commissioner Paul Tagliabue said, "It was an unfortunate accident, but we cannot condone under any circumstances physical contact against our game officials." Meanwhile, debate ensued over the physics of a tossed penalty flag. The NFL would review "the way officials toss flags." Brown sued the NFL for $200 million in 2001 for injuries related to the penalty flag incident. A settlement for about ten percent of the initial claim was reached in 2002. Zeus sat out three seasons of pro football before signing with the Baltimore Ravens in 2003. But the incident is cemented in pro football history and will forever be linked to Cleveland. As Shaw's byline aptly stated on December 20, 1999, "With a Shove, Brown Gives Team Black Eye."

THE NFL WOULD REVIEW "THE WAY OFFICIALS TOSS FLAGS."

78,102 SEE GIANTS SWEEP, 7-4

👎 BIGGEST BUMMERS

THE CATCH AND THE SWEEP

If Indians' fans think the loss to the Florida Marlins in Game Seven of the 1997 World Series hurt, just imagine how Cleveland fans felt about the Tribe's misadventures in the 1954 World Series. That year, the city of Cleveland was feeling extremely confident as the Series approached. The Indians' 111 victories were a record, and they had dethroned the New York Yankees as the American League champs. Spearheading the team's performance was the "Big Four" starting pitching staff of Bob Feller, Early Wynn, Mike Garcia, and Bob Lemon. Garcia and Lemon were '54 All-Stars, along with Bobby Avila, Larry Doby, and Al Rosen. The Giants stayed ahead of the Brooklyn Dodgers by five games to win the National League pennant, and they also had Willie Mays, the National League batting champ in center field. It looked to be an interesting Series, but both bookmakers and fans liked the odds of a Tribe World Series triumph. It might even be a sweep.

Little did they know!

As Indians fans would learn, things don't always go according to plan. Game One was played in New York at the Polo Grounds where the center field wall was 483 feet from home plate. With the score tied 2-2 in the eighth inning, the Tribe's Vic Wertz hit a smash to center field that looked certain to score the two runners on board. In any other park, Wertz's hit would have been a home run. Instead, the Tribe would be victim to perhaps the greatest defensive play in World Series history as Willie Mays made a spectacular over-the-shoulder catch, retiring Wertz. The Indians produced no runs in their half of the eighth, and the game eventually went into extra innings.

In the bottom of the tenth, Bob Lemon gave up a three-run homer to Dusty Rhodes and Game One belonged to the Giants. In Game Two, the Indians' Al Smith hit the first pitch of the game out of the Polo Grounds, but the Tribe lost by a score of 3-1. In Game Three in Cleveland, the Giants held the Indians to four hits, winning 6-2, and now things looked extremely bleak. The Tribe would have to win four straight to take the Series. It wasn't to be, as the Giants were drubbing Cleveland 7-0 after four and a half innings. The Giants won 7-4, sweeping the Series in four straight to the abject horror of Cleveland fans. The Indians' vaunted pitching staff had a Series earned run average of 4.84, giving up 19 earned runs to the Giants' 6. It was a collapse that nobody saw coming, and it lingers in Cleveland sports history as one of the biggest letdowns of all time.

"It all happened so fast, we weren't really aware of how famous it would become. Besides, it was our team that was out, so we weren't all that thrilled about it."

—Indians relief pitcher Don Mossi on
Willie Mays's spectacular catch in Game One

ASK A STUPID QUESTION . . .

After Cavaliers Head Coach Tom Nissalke (1982–1984) was hired, he was asked by a reporter how he pronounced his name. **"Tom,"** he replied.

CURSES!

THE CURSES LIVE ON

Our friends at ESPN.com have ranked the remaining sports curses, and Cleveland has two in the top five. After the Red Sox exorcised the "Curse of the Bambino" by winning the 2004 World Series, ESPN decided it was worth listing the remaining 55 curses in sports. Here are the top five:

1. Curse of the Billy Goat—Chicago Cubs (Last Title: 1908)
2. Curse of the Black Sox—Chicago White Sox (Last Title: 1917)
3. Curse of Paul Brown—Cleveland Browns (Last Title: 1964). The Drive . . . The Fumble . . . Tim Couch. You think legendary coach/owner Paul Brown wanted revenge after getting fired by Art Modell?
4. Curse of Frank Gifford—Philadelphia Eagles (Last Title: 1960)
5. Curse of Chief Wahoo—Cleveland Indians (Last Title: 1948) Sure, Indians fans refer to the Curse of Rocky Colavito, but seriously, get rid of the logo and join the 21st century. The choke in the 1997 Series is underrated.

BAD TRADE

CATCH AND RELEASE

James Timothy "Mudcat" Grant hailed from Lacoochie, Florida and received a tryout from the Indians minor league club in Daytona Beach in the 1950s. The established minor leaguers heckled him and called all sorts of names, including "Mississippi Mudcat," which is another name for a breed of catfish found in the Mississippi River. The name stuck and so did Grant. He pitched for the Indians from 1958 into the 1964 season and compiled a 67-63 record, going 15-9 in 1961. He was traded to the Minnesota Twins for pitcher Lee Stange and infielder George Banks on June 15, 1964.

As Indians' luck would have it, the trade was good for the Mudcat but bad for the Indians. Grant went 21-7 in 1965 and won two World Series games, as the Twins became world champions. In 1973 and 1974, Mudcat teamed-up with Harry Jones on Cleveland Indians TV

broadcasts and became somewhat infamous for his mispronuncia-
tions and fracturing of the English language. Saying "the pitcher's
'repeeetoire' [repertoire] of pitches," or "Mas-silly-on" and "Fos-
toreee-a" for Massillon and Fostoria, Ohio made him an adventure in
radio listening. Mudcat used to have a lounge-act known as "Mudact
and the Kittens" that toured in the off-seasons. In 1965, after the
Twins' World Series triumph, a Minneapolis entertainment critic
wrote that Grant was "unquestionably the best singer in the area to
have won two World Series games this year."

CHARLIE HUSTLE AND THE MULE

Having a Cleveland Indians player selected to the All-Star team
during the dark days of the 1960s and 1970s was always rare and
exciting. It was even more fun when a Tribe All-Star happened
to be a young, up-and-coming player like catcher Ray Fosse.
In only his second year in the American League, Fosse had 16
home runs by the mid-season All-Star break. As Fosse recalls,
"It was kind of a magical first half for me." His efforts were re-
warded with a trip to the 1970 All-Star Game in Cincinnati, Ohio.
As a new major league ball player, Fosse was in heaven when
Cleveland pitcher Sam McDowell invited him to dinner the
night before the game. Their wives accompanied them to dinner with none other than Charlie Hustle himself—Pete Rose of
the Cincinnati Reds. While McDowell and Rose talked baseball,
Fosse took it all in. It was truly a magical season for him and he
would soon be linked with Rose forever in baseball history.

The next day, going into the last half of the ninth inning, the
American League All-Stars had the game well in hand, leading
4-1. But these were the days when All-Star games could still be
considered classics rather than just exhibitions and home-run-
hitting contests. The National League rallied to tie it at 4-4 in
the bottom of the ninth and send the game into extra innings.
In the bottom of the twelfth inning, Rose singled and moved

to second base on a teammate's hit. The next batter, Jim Hickman of the Chicago Cubs, lined a hit to center field. Rose made the turn at third base and headed full-steam toward the plate. The throw from center was not cut off and headed toward the American League's catcher, Ray Fosse. Fosse was playing up the third base line waiting for the throw as Rose bore down on the plate. What happened next would thrust Fosse into fame, but permanently damage his career. Rose hit Fosse "like rain hits the pavement." It was a brutal collision that is replayed to this day. Rose scored the winning run for the National League, and Fosse was taken to the hospital for x-rays.

ROSE HIT FOSSE "LIKE RAIN HITS THE PAVEMENT."

Fosse, nicknamed "Mule" by his teammates for his toughness, was diagnosed with a bruised shoulder but didn't miss any regular season games after the All-Star classic. He should have rested himself, had he known that the swelling around his shoulder hid a fractured bone. Fosse could not lift his left arm above his shoulder without great pain and managed only two home runs in the second half of the 1970 season, yet gutted it out. He never hit more than 12 home runs in his remaining nine years in the American League. "If the play had not occurred," said Fosse in an interview with the *San Francisco Chronicle*, who knows what direction my career would have taken? Could I have hit 25 to 30 (home runs) consistently every year?"

Rose explained his actions. "He was about two feet in front of the plate. If I slid in there, I could have broken both legs. If I slid head first, I could have broken my neck." Broken instead was the potentially great career of a young Indian catcher. Still, there is some justice in how events turned out. When Pete Rose was sentenced to jail for tax evasion, he went to a prison in Marion, Illinois—the hometown of Ray Fosse. According to Fosse, "the folks back home found that a joyous occasion."

*"I just wanted to get to that plate as quickly
as I can. Besides, nobody told me they changed it
to girl's softball between third and home."*

—Pete Rose

DUBIOUS DRAFT

CAVS MIGHT HAVE HAD A WORTHY PLAYER

Ownership of the Cleveland Cavaliers changed hands in June 1980 when original owner Nick Mileti sold his interest in the team to Ted Stepien. Around the same time, the Cavaliers were making Chad Kinch, a 6'-4" guard from the University of North Carolina–Charlotte, the 22nd overall pick in the 1980 NBA Draft. Kinch made a 1977 final four NCAA tournament appearance that got him some national exposure, but it's unclear what the Cavaliers saw in him. He normally appears on lists of the Cavaliers' worst draft picks, having had the proverbial "cup of coffee" with the Cavs, playing in only 29 games. On February 7, 1981, he was traded to the Dallas Mavericks.

The worst part of the deal was how the Cavaliers obtained the first-round pick in 1980 to choose Kinch. During the 1979–1980 season, the Los Angeles Lakers sent forward Don Ford and a 1980 first-round pick to Cleveland for guard Butch Lee and the Cavaliers' first round draft pick in 1982. Obviously the Cavs used the 1980 pick on Kinch. The 1982 first-round pick acquired by the Lakers happened to be the first pick overall, since the Cavs occupied the NBA basement with a 15-67 record.

The Lakers were ecstatic, as they benefited from the Cavs' abysmal season and the resulting first pick. They grabbed forward James Worthy from the University of North Carolina Tarheels. Lots could be written about James Worthy, but his coach, Pat Riley, said it best after Worthy retired after the 1993–1994 NBA season, "I don't think there has been or will be a better small forward than James." His nickname, "Big Game James," says it all. Sadly, Chad Kinch did not continue in the NBA beyond his 1981 stint with the Mavericks. He died in 1994 from AIDS-related complications.

DYSFUNCTIONAL FAMILY AFFAIR

The Indians organization was the dumping ground for two ex-Yankee pitchers who were part of one of the most bizarre incidents in baseball marital history. In fact, an ESPN.com online poll ranked this incident in the top 10 most shocking moments in baseball history, along with the Giants and Dodgers leaving New York and Bill Buckner's infamous error in Game Six of the 1986 World Series. On June 12, 1973, Yankee pitcher Mike Kekich was traded to the Cleveland Indians for Tribe pitcher Lowell Palmer. No big deal . . . swaps of little known players happen frequently in baseball. Kekich lasted the season and was released by the Tribe on March 28, 1974 before the season started. Enter ex-Yankee pitcher Fritz Peterson, a finesse pitcher with a 109-106 lifetime record and a 20-game win season in 1970. The Tribe gave up first baseman Chris Chambliss and pitchers Dick Tidrow and Cecil Upshaw for him on April 27, 1974. The Indians were looking for pitching and were forced into parting with its rising star, Chambliss.

What caused the buzz over the Peterson-Chambliss trade was actually the reason for Mike Kekich trade the year before. In early March 1973, Kekich and Peterson had shown up at the Yankees' spring training site and announced to their teammates they had swapped families. No, not wives, but entire families! Even the pet family dogs were traded—the Kekiches' terrier for the Petersons' poodle. Needless to say, the Yankees' front office was less-than-thrilled over the announcement of the family swap on the eve of the 1973 season. They dispatched Kekich and his (er, Peterson's) family to Cleveland, while Peterson and his (er, Kekich's family) remained in New York. The life-swapping

> # *"We didn't do anything sneaky or lecherous. There isn't anything smutty about this."*
>
> —Susan Kekich

event took its toll on both pitchers. Kekich finished his career with Seattle in 1977 and broke up with Marilyn Peterson within a year of the swap. Fritz Peterson had a decent 1975 season for the Indians, going 14-8, but exited the major leagues after going 2-6 for three teams in 1976. He eventually married Susan Kekich and they had four more children together. Baseball lore has long identified left-handed pitchers as unique creatures possessing flaky personalities, often exhibiting weird and unconventional behavior. Were Kekich and Peterson lefties or righties? Look it up, you won't be surprised.

ONLY IN CLEVELAND

Beyond Pain

At various low spells in their 35-year history, when lackluster play, losing records, and fan apathy were the order of the day, the Cleveland Cavaliers were referred to as the Cleveland "Cadavers."

DUBIOUS DRAFT

ANOTHER ONE FOR THE MEDICAL FILES

There was no debate leading up to the 2000 NFL Draft for the Cleveland Browns. They would be selecting a defensive player from Penn State. The question was, which one? Would it be linebacker LaVar Arrington or defensive end Courtney Brown? The Browns went for the impressive 6'-4", 290-pound specimen and planned on his presence at defensive end for years to come. Instead of leading the league in quarterback sacks, Brown probably set some kind of record for games missed due to injuries. He made it through the 2000 season with the normal complement of bumps and bruises. But over the four-year period 2001-2004, he sat out 33 games. Here's the medical report on the No. 1 pick in the 2000 draft:

August 31, 2001—Torn posterior cruciate ligament in right knee in the final preseason game. Misses six regular season games.

December 2, 2001—Ankle sprain in eleventh game of the regular season. Misses the remaining five games.

September 8, 2002—Neck bruise in the opening game against Kansas City. Misses one game.

November 24, 2002—Bruised left knee against the New Orleans Saints. Misses two games. Later in the season, micro-fracture surgery is performed to help rebuild cartilage in the knee.

December 8, 2003—Ruptured right biceps tendon. Misses final three games.

February 2004—Arthroscopic knee surgery. Will be ready to start the 2004 season.

September 20, 2004—Torn Lisfranc ligament in left foot. Misses final 14 games of the regular season.

Brown was released in March 2005 and signed on with the Denver Broncos. All totaled, Courtney Brown collected $26 million in salary from the Browns over five seasons and used his health insurance plan almost as much.

THE HAWK LANDS IN CLEVELAND

It was 1969. Indians' season attendance below the magic million mark as another sub-.500 seasons had the Tribe struggling for fan interest, a common theme of those years. General Manager Gabe Paul thought he had the cure for Cleveland's ills, but the medicine would be costly. He hatched a deal with the Boston Red Sox on April 19, 1969, that sent starting pitcher Sonny Siebert, catcher Joe Azcue, and reliever Vicente Romo to Beantown for first baseman Ken "Hawk" Harrelson and pitchers Juan Pizzaro and Dick Ellsworth. The marquee player in the deal was Harrelson, *Sporting News*'s Player of the Year, whose protruding nose had earned him the nickname "Hawk." He had developed quite a following in Boston, not only because of his 1968 season of 35 home runs, 109 RBIs, and a .275 average, but also because his stylishly long hair, trendy attire, and rock-star life-style appealed to young fans. Paul had to cough up even more cash when the Hawk refused to report to Cleveland until he had a new and more expensive contract. He was given his own television show, called "The Hawks Nest," and rumor had it he wanted a helicopter to fly him from his Lakewood Gold Coast apartment to Municipal Stadium for home games. Cleveland had a celebrity star whose 1969 stats weren't all that bad, either—30 home runs and 92 RBIs. Ah, but this is Cleveland, Hawk, and strange things happen even to celebrities.

In spring training the following year, a slide into second base during an exhibition game against the Oakland A's snapped the Hawk's right claw. When his broken ankle healed, the Hawk left the nest and returned to the Tribe in September 1970, playing in only 17 games. Fed up with the trademark fan apathy in Cleveland, Harrelson wanted out the next season, but a trade didn't develop. After playing only 52 games with a weakened leg, Harrelson grounded himself. He retired from professional baseball on June 21, 1971, only to try the pro golf tour and then land in the Chicago White Sox TV broadcast booth, where he has been perched for the last 16 seasons.

And of course, Sonny Siebert would have looked good for the ailing Tribe had he remained an Indian. He went 64-52 over the next five seasons.

CONSPICUOUS CONSUMPTION

When Akron St. Vincent-St. Mary high school basketball phenom Lebron James received a $50,000 Hummer vehicle for his eighteenth birthday, it caused then Cleveland Cavaliers' assistant coach Jerry Eaves to remark, **"When I was a teenager, I got a red 1972 Pinto."**

THE SECOND COMING

Ask a Clevelander to define the "Second Coming" and they'll tell you: the 1999 return of the Cleveland Browns. It would be interesting to return to the end of the fatal 1995 Browns season and see the reaction of Browns fans if they'd been promised a billionaire owner and a wheeler-dealer team president to build a new Browns' team in 1999. How about adding a playoff berth in three years; a Super Bowl to come in five. Fate would finally smile on Browns Town; the shabby treatment of 1995 would be redressed! Well, it actually happened. That is, the billionaire owner and wheeler-dealer president part actually happened.

In retrospect, neither Lerner's money nor Policy's incessant spinning could overcome the bad breaks and questionable decisions that became the hallmarks of the Second Coming. The new team squandered its regular and bonus picks in the 1999 Draft. First-pick Tim Couch, the Kentucky quarterback with questionable arm strength, was out of the NFL by 2004. He suffered a sprained ankle in the next-to-last game of the 1999 season and sat out the season finale. In the 2000 season he fractured his throwing hand in practice and missed the season's remaining nine games. In 2001, Paul Hilton "Butch" Davis was lured from the University of Miami by Carmen Policy to coach the team. Yet Davis's first draft proved to be a bust for the Browns, as the first four picks—Gerard Warren, Quincy Morgan, James Jackson, and Anthony Henry—all exited via free agency, trades, or outright releases. The fifth-round pick, linebacker Jeremiah Pharms, never made it to his first training camp. He was charged with pistol-whipping and shooting a drug dealer over the purchase of $1,500 worth of marijuana. The Browns released him.

If 2002 wasn't a star-crossed season, nothing was. The team's only legitimate All-Pro player, linebacker Jamir Miller, tore his Achilles tendon in a meaningless preseason exhibition game against the Minnesota Vikings. He never returned to the NFL. Another linebacker, Dwayne Rudd, cost the club its home-opener against Kansas City when he tossed his helmet in jubilation, thinking he had sacked the quarterback; instead he was penalized, giving the Chiefs new life. A sore throwing arm prevented quarterback Tim Couch from starting the 2002 season, yet he returned in the third game, only to be knocked out with a concussion in the  fifth game against the Baltimore Ravens. In an ill-advised postgame interview, he whined about the fans not supporting him. A broken leg in the last game of the season eliminated him from the Browns' first playoff appearance since their return.

Sadly, team owner Alfred Lerner died on October 23, 2002, after battling brain cancer. Despite the adversity, the Browns traveled to Pittsburgh on January 5, 2003 to face the Steelers in their first playoff game since the Second Coming. If this game did anything, it seemed to solidify the suspicion that the Browns were cursed. With quarterback Kelly Holcomb passing for 429 yards, the Browns went into free-fall after leading the Steelers 24-7 with eight minutes left in the third quarter and losing the game 36-33. Butch Davis overruled his defensive coordinator, Foge Fazio, on how to defend Pittsburgh in the fourth quarter. It could be argued that there was no defense—the Steelers scored 22 points in the final period.

During the 2003 and 2004 seasons, running back William Green tangled himself in drug, drinking, and domestic violence traps; wide receiver Kevin Johnson was unexplainably released; and 2004 first round-pick Kellen Winslow broke his leg in the season's second game against Dallas. Head Coach Butch Davis "resigned" with five games left in 2004. Early in 2005, Winslow ensured his second straight NFL sabbatical by damaging his body in an unsupervised spin on his powerful brand new motorcycle.

The Browns' second time around was supposed to be different. Cleveland was more than deserving of catching a break, or so the logic went. While many were expecting a dynasty, some would say that what we've really received is our destiny.

DUBIOUS DRAFT

WE DRAFTED THE WRONG KING

In the 1991 NFL Draft, the Cleveland Browns selected offensive lineman Ed King from Auburn University with their second-round pick. Still available in Round Two was Southern Mississippi quarterback Brett Favre. Favre has been named the NFL's Most Valuable Player three times (1995, 1996, and 1997) and led his team to a Super Bowl victory in 1997. King lasted two years with the Browns.

MAJOR LEAGUE MISERY INDEX

Jim Caple at ESPN.com is a genius. He invented the MLB Misery Index. It's a system that measures two types of baseball fan misery: despair, produced by losing seasons; and pain, brought on by agonizing ends to winning seasons. Our Cleveland Indians rank second in this index behind the Montreal Expos (now the Washington Nationals). The higher the score, the worse the misery. The Expos scored 50, Cleveland scored 44, followed by the Chicago Cubs and White Sox.

TOUGH LUCK

BREAKING BALL, BROKEN ARM

You need three things to win in baseball: pitching, pitching, and more pitching. The Indians were in the market for more pitching during the 1997 season. Tribe GM John Hart pulled the trigger on a deal that sent pitchers Danny Graves, Scott Winchester, Jim Powell, and infielder Damien Jackson to the Cincinnati Reds for veteran left-hander John Smiley and infielder Jeff Branson on July 31, 1997. The principals in the deal were Graves and Smiley. While Graves was an up and coming reliever/closer, Smiley was expected to be that left-handed starter for whom the Tribe was so desperate. But this deal turned south on the Tribe within two months. First Smiley went on the disabled list with elbow problems in August. Then, while warming up for a September 20 start against the Royals in Kansas City, Smiley fractured the humerus bone in his pitching arm. Bullpen coach Luis Isaac said, "He went to throw his first curveball and his armed snapped. It sounded like dry wood breaking. He grabbed his arm and started screaming." Fellow pitcher Jason Jacome said, "You could see the upper part of his arm was sort of deformed. We all knew something was really wrong. My stomach turned." So did the stomachs of the Indians front office as they came up empty in their search for pitching, especially since it cost them Graves. Smiley never made it back from the unfortunate injury. Graves went on to have a solid career as a closer with the Reds before his release in 2005.

Sipe is set to become a N.J. General today

TRUMPED

After a spectacular Cleveland Browns' career as the leader of the "Kardiac Kids" (1978–1983), quarterback Brian Sipe bolted from the NFL for the same job with the Donald Trump–owned New Jersey Generals of the United States Football League. Although a good move for Sipe financially, the Browns suffered in 1984 as Paul McDonald filled the quarterback spot and led the team to a 5-11 record. McDonald was drafted in 1980 as a back-up to Sipe with a bit of a quarterback controversy developing in 1982. The Browns would maneuver to get the rights to Bernie Kosar in 1985, since McDonald was not the team's answer at quarterback.

IN SEARCH OF PITCHING

At the time the Indians traded 17-year-old minor league prospect Pedro Guerrero to the Los Angeles Dodgers, they were in need of left-handed bullpen help. In exchange, they received Bruce Ellingsen, who had shown promise in the Dodgers' minor league system. Ellingsen didn't stay with the big league club but was optioned to the minors after the deal was made on April 3, 1974. When he returned to the Indians later in the season, it was only for a short time, and he never saw a major league mound again.

It turned out much different for Guerrero, a Cuban ball player signed by the Tribe in 1973. The one-time property of the Indians became arguably one of the best hitters in baseball during the 1980s. He was described by baseball writer Bill James as "the best hitter God has made in a long time." In Game Six of the 1981 World Series, Guerrero drove in five runs to help the Dodgers clinch the Series from the Yankees. In 1984, he became the highest paid Dodger at that point, with a five-year contract worth $7 million. The Tribe sure could have used his bat during the 1980s. Except for 1986 when an injury caused him to miss most of the season, his Dodger numbers from 1980 through 1987 proved his stature as a consistent .300 hitter.

Once out of Major League Baseball, Pedro lived an adventuresome life. He was suspended from the Mexican League in 1999 for unknown reasons, and he may be one of the few people on whom O.J. Simpson called the police. Guerrero was seeing a girlfriend of O.J.'s (after O.J.'s murder charge acquittal), so O.J called the police on them. Drugs were involved and details are sketchy, but at least Guerrero was described as the "former Dodger" and not the "former Indian." Thank goodness for small favors.

BIGGEST BUMMERS
THE SHOT

It ranks right up there in Cleveland sports crushers with the Drive, the Fumble, and Game Seven. The Cavaliers are the victim here, and the disappointment came at the hands of Michael Jordan and the Chicago Bulls during the first round of the NBA playoffs in 1989. The Cavs finished the year six games behind the Central Division winners, the Detroit Pistons, and ahead of the Bulls by ten, winning a record 57 games. The Bulls just made it into the playoffs as the sixth seed in the Eastern Conference. The Cavs and Bulls evenly exchanged wins and losses over the first four games to force a deciding game five. Because the Cavaliers were the better team that year,

Cavaliers bounced from playoffs

Jordan's heroics ruin Ehlo's effort

having swept the Bulls in the regular season, and because Game Five was in Cleveland at the Coliseum, the prospects of a Cleveland victory over Michael Jordan and the Bulls were good.

The basketball world knew of Jordan, his slam-dunk talent, and his spectacular 1988–1989 season. But the Bulls had only been victorious in one playoff series with Jordan, and there was doubt about his ability to deliver in the clutch. All doubts were erased on May 7, 1989, at the close of Game Five. The Cavaliers held a 100-99 lead in the final seconds of the game before a raucous Richfield Coliseum crowd. They could taste the sweetness of revenge for the Bulls eliminating the Cavaliers from the playoffs a year earlier. Once again, the match-up was the Cavaliers' Craig Ehlo on Michael Jordan. With the lead changing five times in the last 90 seconds, both Ehlo and Jordan were putting on a scoring and defensive show. But in the final three seconds, the course of two basketball franchises was cast. Jordan received the ball and floated a double-pump shot over the outstretched arm of Ehlo at the buzzer. In it went. The Bulls had eliminated the Cavaliers from the playoffs again. More significantly, the Bulls eventually went on to win six NBA titles in two "three-peat" periods separated by two seasons. The Cavs' fortunes went downhill, as trades involving Ron Harper and others weakened a playoff-caliber team.

THE "SHOT" AND THE HYPE SURROUNDING IT PROPELLED MICHAEL JORDAN ON HIS RIDE TO SUPER-STARDOM.

The "Shot" and the hype surrounding it propelled Michael Jordan on his ride to super-stardom. According to NBA.com, fans responding to the "Greatest Shots of the Playoffs" poll have selected the shot that beat the Cavs in Game Five of the 1989 Eastern Conference First Round playoffs as the greatest shot ever taken in playoff history. Actually, the Cavaliers have had the displeasure of other Jordan killer shots. On May 17, 1993, Jordan killed the Cavs with another buzzer-beating fade away jump shot to eliminate them from the Eastern Conference Semifinal playoffs. And in a regular season game on January 31, 2002, Jordan dropped yet another buzzer-beater on the Cavs while a member of the Washington Wizards.

WHO'S IN CHARGE HERE?

TOUGH LUCK

Some baseball fans may recall the 1980 playoffs when the Yankees' third base coach, Mike Ferraro, waived Willie Randolph home only to be cut down at home plate. The Yankees lost the American League Championship to the Kansas City Royals in three straight games, and Boss Steinbrenner was plenty mad. In its never-ending quest for success, the Cleveland Indians' management must have liked what they saw in Ferraro because they hired him to manage the Indians on November 4, 1982, granting him a two-year contract. A month before he was hired, Ferraro had signed a three-year coaching deal with the Yankees, but Steinbrenner let him out of that deal. Things started out on an unfortunate note for the new manager as he underwent surgery for a cancerous kidney in February 1983, but he rallied to take charge when the season started. But a combination of Ferraro's recovery from surgery and the reality of running the Cleveland Indians, not the New York Yankees, did him in. He only made it through 100 games and was fired on July 31, 1983. It was reported that Ferraro was unhappy with the way the team was playing, and the players felt Ferraro didn't communicate well.

Reporting for the *Plain Dealer* at the time, sportswriter Terry Pluto relates a story that typified the season for Ferraro. In a game against the Kansas City Royals, the Indians ran off the field after a double play, thinking they had made the third out. But the double play produced only two outs. Years later, Mike Hargrove related to Pluto, "It was the kind of double play that usually ends an inning. I caught the ball at first [for what was thought to be the third out] and rolled it to the mound and the whole team just followed me to the dugout. They had to call us back on the field. I told [coach] Johnny Goryl, 'That has to change Ferraro's mind about us having no leaders. I led the whole team right off the field.'" The Tribe replaced Ferraro with Pat Corrales, the manager of the Philadelphia Phillies who had been fired on July 18. Corrales was canned because the Phillies weren't playing up to their potential, according to their General Manager, Paul Owens. The Phillies were in first place at the time of the firing. As it goes in baseball, as well as with the Tribe, managers are hired to be fired. But at least give the guy a season!

> ### *"The contract will give Mike some stability. The players know that he is going to be around."*
>
> Indians President Gabe Paul upon hiring Mike Ferraro

AND MODEST, TOO

With a losing 1984 season already in progress, Browns head coach Sam Rutigliano told those assembled at his weekly press conference that he was **"good for the city of Cleveland both as a coach and a person,"** further stating, **"I think you're all lucky that I'm here."** Coming on the heels of a 17-16 loss to the New England Patriots on October 8th, a game the Browns should have won, Sam also remarked he **"wasn't going anywhere."** On October 22, 1984, Sam was fired as head coach of the Browns.

They can't hold their beer

SAY IT WITH SHOWERS

Referees were making up the rules as they went along. Fans were venting their mixed-up emotions over a bad call, having lost their beloved team for three years, and getting a lousy expansion team in return. It all came to a head on December 16, 2001 in a game that is known as "The Bottle Game" against the Jacksonville Jaguars.

Victories were a precious commodity to the three-year old Browns' franchise, and the prospect of one was worth dying for, or at least going to jail for, in the case of some fans. So when Browns quarterback Tim Couch spiked the ball at the Jags' nine yard line to halt the clock with 48 seconds to go and trailing 15-10, things looked promising. But the referees were conferring about something, and that is always a worrisome sight. Sure enough, they announced to the crowd that in the play *previous* to the spiked ball, receiver Quincy Morgan did not have possession of the ball and therefore did not attain a first down.

As the Browns players and coaches protested not only the referee's decision, but the review of the play that occurred *before* Couch spiked the ball, the Cleveland Dawg Pound section erupted by throwing filled and unfilled plastic water bottles and other items onto the field. The bottle tossing became epidemic throughout the stadium, while players and referees fled for the safety of the locker rooms, dodging the bottles and debris as they ran. With only 48 seconds remaining in such a riotous atmosphere, most fans thought the game was over. In their inimitable wisdom, the NFL ordered the teams out to the field for the final 48 seconds. The national spotlight shone on our city once again, but it wasn't for our team's achievements. One journalist wrote, "Just about the time when this city starts to convince us it's not the Mistake on the Lake, something happens to embarrass Cleveland all over again." Browns President Carmen Policy, who never saw a microphone he didn't like, further alienated the rest of the country by saying, "I don't think Cleveland will take a black eye from this. I like the fact that our fans care." Many Browns fans like the fact that Carmen is now making wine in California.

> ### *"It wasn't pleasant. I wouldn't suggest anything like that. But it wasn't World War III."*
> Browns owner Al Lerner after the bottle-throwing
> incident at Cleveland Browns Stadium

Fans pelt field with bottles after reversal

IF IT AIN'T BROKE . . .

In the 1988 off-season, the Indians wanted shortstop Julio Franco to switch to second base. Julio refused and was dealt to the Texas Rangers on December 6, 1988 for first baseman Pete O'Brien, outfielder Odibe McDowell, and second baseman Jerry Browne. Pete O'Brien left the Tribe after one season, McDowell was traded to Atlanta in 1989, and Browne (nicknamed "Governor" after then California governor Jerry Brown) played well for two seasons and left as a free agent in 1991. What about Julio? In 1991 he won the American League batting title with a .341 batting average. He returned briefly to Cleveland in 1996–1997. As of the start of the 2005 Major League Baseball season, Julio was playing with the Atlanta Braves at 46 years old and still a productive hitter! Oh, by the way, Julio came to Cleveland in 1982 for Von Hayes, a very promising Cleveland hitting outfielder. This was not a popular trade at the time. Hayes finished his 12-year career with a lifetime .267 average and 696 runs batted-in. In any event, the Tribe would have been better served by leaving Julio at shortstop in 1989 and just watching him do his thing.

That's Using Your Head

On May 26, 1993, as the Indians played the Texas Rangers at Municipal Stadium, Tribe batter Carlos Martinez hit a towering drive toward Rangers outfielder Jose Canseco. As Canseco went up to grab the fly ball, it went through his glove, hit him on the head, and bounced over the fence for a home run. Canseco said later that the replays would have him on ESPN for a month.

TOUGH LUCK

MACK SURVIVES HIS OWN ATTACK

On Tuesday, June 27, 1989, Browns fullback Kevin Mack attended his normal off-season workout session along with his teammates. He was an important part of the Browns playoff teams of the late 1980s and had produced a 1,104-yard rushing season in 1985. The following day, police arrested him and two companions at East 55th Street and Scovil Avenue on charges of drug possession and aggravated drug trafficking. What made this so hard to believe was that Mack, the 6-foot, 224-pound battering ram was an unassuming person. Browns tight-end Ozzie Newsome told reporters he was shocked. "Kevin is such a quiet guy, nobody had a clue."

As the story unfolded, it became known that Mack lacked self-confidence despite his on-the-field exploits. Running mate Earnest Byner constantly was doing things to boost Mack's fragile self-esteem but couldn't prevent his fall into drug addiction. Mack served a 30-day prison term after pleading guilty to illegal drug use. He also had minor surgery on his knee and his comeback prospects were bleak. With hard work and the help of Browns assistant conditioning

"Kevin is such a quiet guy, nobody had a clue."

coach Gary Wroblewski, Mack was ready to play by season's end. His head-down, four-yard TD run with 39 seconds against the Houston Oilers clinched the AFC Central Division title for the Browns. A dramatic moment indeed. Mack's teammates swarmed around him in support—and gratitude. Considering where his drug addiction may have taken him, bulling his way into the end zone against the Houston defense was just a Sunday afternoon walk in the park.

THESE BOOTS ARE MADE FOR . . . STOPPIN' BULLETS

Anytime a rookie makes it to the big leagues you can be sure he'll do just about anything to remain there. And so it was, on September 29, 2004, after starting the game against the Kansas City Royals, that Oklahoma native Kyle Denney didn't flinch when given his rookie hazing assignment by the Tribe veterans. A huge Oklahoma fan, Denney was given a rival University of Southern California cheerleader outfit—blond wig and white go-go boots—to wear on the trip to Minneapolis. Dutifully, Denney hopped aboard the team bus at Kansas City's Kaufman Stadium for the trip to the airport. Enroute, some deranged person fired a gunshot at the Cleveland team bus. The bullet pierced the side of the bus where Denney was riding and came to rest in his right calf. A gunshot wound is nothing to make light of, but fortunately in this case Denney was spared a serious wound. Thanks to the side of the bus and the imitation leather go-go boots Denney was sporting (USC cheerleaders don't actually wear boots, by the way), the bullet was slowed enough to cause only a flesh wound. Team trainers on the bus removed the bullet, and Denney received minor medical treatment at the hospital. The next day at a news conference, Denney said "I was never so glad to have a USC thing on."

When Denney got to spring training in 2005, he was hit in the knee by a thrown bat, didn't make the Indians' big league roster, and missed the minor league Buffalo Bison's Opening Day. Later he went on the disabled list for a month with elbow problems. If this weren't enough, he was then hit in the head by a line drive off the bat of Durham's Joey Gaithright. Denney suffered a concussion and was hospitalized for several days. Bisons Manager Marty Brown told reporters, "It looks positive. He [Denney] was very coherent and called me a name I can't repeat. He said this hurt worse than the gunshot wound." A tough year for Kyle Denney.

ONLY IN CLEVELAND

Great Names

In what has to be one of the most celebrated "trades of names," the Browns swapped wide receivers with the New Orleans Saints on August 26, 1974. They sent four-year veteran wide receiver Fair Hooker to the Saints for another wide receiver, Jubilee Dunbar. The trade was probably a "fair" one for both teams as both Dunbar and Hooker had lackluster seasons for their new teams and soon exited football. Hooker's notoriety came on the first Monday Night Football broadcast, September 21, 1970, when ABC announcer Don Meredith exclaimed, "Isn't Fair Hooker a great name?" For that reason alone, the Browns should have kept him.

HOCKEY IN CLEVELAND

What is it with professional hockey in Cleveland? After the love affair between the "old" American Hockey League (AHL) Cleveland Barons and the city from 1937 to 1973, it seems that the pro game hasn't struck a deep chord with the community. Nick Mileti owned the original Barons as well as the cozy Cleveland Arena on Euclid Avenue at the time of their demise. With the opening of his Coliseum in Richfield Township, he abandoned the Arena and eventually moved the Barons to Jacksonville, Florida because they couldn't co-exist with Mileti's new World Hockey Association (WHA) franchise known as the Cleveland Crusaders. The Crusaders lasted five years (1972-1976) and moved to St. Paul, Minnesota to become the Minnesota Fighting Saints. In 1976, Cleveland finally received a National Hockey League (NHL) franchise and took the name of the original Barons. But the lure and tradition of the old AHL Barons could not be duplicated.

On June 14, 1978, the NHL re-incarnated Barons were laid to rest, merging with the Minnesota North Stars. Minor league hockey returned to Cleveland in the form of the Lumberjacks of the International Hockey League (IHL) in the early 1990s. They were lost in the dissolution of the IHL in 2001. But never fear, the Barons came back, this time as a minor league farm team of the NHL San Jose Sharks in the re-constituted American Hockey League. The more things change, the more they stay the same. Cleveland was meant to have the Barons, even if their logo is a goofy mixture of a Baron and a Shark called "Slap Shark."

NOT A WYNNING PICK

It was April 2000 and the "new" Browns had finished their inaugural season in 1999. Ready to make their sixth-round pick in the 2000 draft, the Browns' brain trust decided to take a chance on someone to back-up their franchise quarterback, Tim Couch, whom they'd drafted with the draft's first pick a year earlier. With the 183rd overall pick, they selected a strong-armed quarterback from Southwest Texas State, Spergon Wynn. Later in round six, the New England Patriots selected quarterback Tom Brady from the University of Michigan with the 199th overall pick. Brady eventually took over from the in-jured Drew Bledsoe in New England and led the Pats to Super Bowl championships in 2002, 2004, and 2005. In 2002 and 2004, he was named the Super Bowl Most Valuable Player.

Cleveland shared the dunce cap with the San Francisco 49'ers, the New York Jets, the Pittsburgh Steelers, and the St. Louis Rams. Each drafted a quarterback in the 2000 NFL Draft ahead of Brady. Wynn appeared in seven games for the Browns in 2000, completing 22 of 54 passes for 167 yards and 1 interception. He was traded to the Minnesota Vikings before the 2001 season, where he played in three games, completing 48 of 98 passes for 418 yards, 1 touchdown, and 6 interceptions. In 2004, Wynn kept going farther north as one of the British Columbia Lions' back-up quarterbacks.

CURSES!

ONLY IN CLEVELAND

Finley Hit Hard

On April 1, 2002, pitcher Chuck Finley was getting ready to make his first start of the new major league season for the Cleveland Indians. On a road trip to Southern California to play his former team, the California Angels, Finley, whose off-season home is in Newport Beach, spent some time with his family. After an evening dinner with his wife, former B-movie actress Tawney Kitaen, Finley began the drive home—with a little help from his wife. With a dinnertime argument still raging, Kitaen began kicking Finley with her high heels and pressing down on his foot that was on the accelerator pedal. For good measure, Kitaen twisted her husband's ear and scratched his face. Finley filed assault charges and followed those up with divorce papers on April 4. Kitaen did some pitching of her own as she hurled charges of pot smoking and avoiding major league drug testing. Finley was so shaken by the events, he missed his first start of the season. Not only was 2002 Finley's last season with the Tribe, it was his swan song in the major league. Finley finished the year, and his career, with the St. Louis Cardinals.

Sports Illustrated Cover Jinx

RYAN GETS IT AGAIN

Once again, Cleveland Browns quarterback Frank Ryan graced the cover of *Sports Illustrated*, this time on September 27, 1965. The cover by-line is, "Dr. Ryan of the Browns—How Smart is Too Smart?" and the article by Jack Olsen looks inside the mind of the Cleveland Ph.D. quarterback. True to form, the Browns, then the reigning NFL champs were blown away by the St. Louis Cardinals 49-13 the Sunday after the issue hit the newsstands.

LOSING THE LOTTERY

Early in 1966, a University of Southern California baseball player was ruled ineligible for college baseball after it was determined he had signed a major league contract with the Atlanta Braves. On April 3, 1966, major league baseball held a lottery for the rights to this player. Only three teams were permitted to participate—the New York Mets, Philadelphia Phillies, and Cleveland Indians. Of course, Cleveland didn't win the contest; the Mets won the player's rights and a whole lot more. In the luck of the draw, the Indians lost a chance to claim right-handed pitcher, Tom Seaver. Seaver pitched in the National League for the Mets and Cincinnati Reds and in the American League for the Chicago White Sox and the Boston Red Sox. He wound up his career in a small town in New York—Cooperstown.

SO THAT'S WHAT IT TAKES TO WIN BALLGAMES

Indians General Manager Gabe Paul offered this observation about Joe Adcock, his manager of only one season before being fired by Paul. **"He had no imagination. I saw him throw away a Marilyn Monroe calendar just because it was December 31st."**

CURSES!

BIGGEST BUMMERS
RED RIGHT 88

Red Right 88. Two words and a number that Browns fans don't want to hear. They conjure up bad memories of a pass meant for tight end Ozzie Newsome that ended up instead in the arms of Oakland defender Mike Davis. The Kardiac Kids were trailing the Raiders 14-12 with 49 seconds left in the 1980 Divsional Playoff game, and they had the ball on the Raiders 13-yard line. On the sideline, the Browns coaching staff huddled with quarterback Brian Sipe on their strategy for the upcoming third and nine play call. Should they run the ball to get a better angle on a field goal? The sub-zero temperature and swirling lakefront winds made for treacherous kicking conditions. Rutigliano made the call for Red Right 88. As Sipe turned to trot back to the huddle, Rutigliano reminded him that if the receiver wasn't open, he should "throw it to the blonde in the mezzanine." Sipe launched the pass to Newsome, but Davis stepped in front of him and picked it off. It was ironic because, as Raider teammates would later reveal, Davis was known to have the worst hands of anyone in their defensive secondary.

To some who retell this story, the Browns had thus missed a spot in the Super Bowl; in fact, a win would have advanced them only to the AFC Championship Game. But the pain of losing gripped Cleveland for days after the game. The Kardiac Kids' trademark during the 1980 season was to pull rabbits out of the hat. They finished the regular season 11-5, with 12 of 16 games decided by 7 points or less. The frozen faithful at Municipal Stadium refused to believe that Sipe's pass had been intercepted. Finally realizing that the dream was over, nearly 80,000 fans filed silently out of the stadium as darkness began to fall. Even without the wind chill of -18 degrees, they were too numb to talk.

"Throw it to the blonde in the mezzanine."

Kardiac arrest

Browns' season ends on questionable call of 'Red Right 88' pass

ARE WE HAPPY YET?

In 2005, *ESPN: The Magazine* conducted a survey on fan satisfaction involving teams in Major League Baseball, the National Football League, and the National Basketball Association. Dubbed the "Ultimate Standings," the survey is a subjective exercise of home fans' reaction to their local ownership, how the team relates to the fans, affordability of tickets, stadium experience, players' on-the-field effort, coaching, and championships won or expected to be won. A measure of objectivity is thrown in for wins-per-dollars spent by fans to watch their teams play. The Browns came in dead last: 90th out of 90 major league franchises.

TEARING YOUR HEART OUT

The 1989 NFL Draft was a gamble for the Cleveland Browns. Under General Manager Ernie Accorsi and new head coach Bud Carson, the Browns practically depleted their draft to move up to take running back Eric Metcalf. Then they traded their 1990 first-round pick so they could draft Auburn receiver Lawyer Tillman. Worst of all, they practically gave away the "heart and soul" of the 1980s Cleveland Browns, Earnest Byner. He was traded to the Washington Redskins for obscure 5'-9", 173-pound running back Mike Oliphant. The Browns claimed to have liked Oliphant in the 1988 draft but Washington picked him. They saw him as a speedy back who could return kicks, but wasn't that a description of Eric Metcalf? There was speculation that Byner was sent packing because of the baggage he carried as a result of his infamous fumble in the 1988 AFC Championship Game. Byner went on to help the Redskins win a Super Bowl in 1992 and was named one of the "70 Greatest Redskins" in 2002 honoring the team's seventieth anniversary. Oliphant appeared in 14 games for Cleveland in 1989 and rushed for 97 yards. By the middle of the 1991 season, he was out of football.

On the day Byner was traded, Ernie Accorsi was asked who would take over the role of the spiritual leader—the "heart and soul"—of the team. "I don't know," he said. "We've got a lot of souls out there." Byner would come back to the Browns in 1994 and was here for the ugly, final season of 1995. While the fans remembered the fumble of 1988, they nevertheless embraced him. They knew that trading him away to Washington was a blunder.

LIP SERVICE

DAWGS AND FIRE HYDRANTS

"I haven't been back to Cleveland since 'The Drive.' Actually, when I was there, the fire hydrants were all painted orange with my number on them. I just wonder if the paint has worn off yet." John Elway, upon his return to Northern Ohio for induction to the Pro Football Hall of Fame in August 2004.

ONLY IN CLEVELAND

Oh, This Is Baseball

In 1983 and 1984, the Indians hired former Browns wide receiver Reggie Rucker to team with announcer Joe Tait on the team's television broadcasts. It seemed odd that a former NFL player would provide commentary for baseball broadcast, but remember we're talking about the Indians here. Rucker once opined that when there is a runner on third base, he'd move an outfielder behind the catcher in case there was a wild pitch. The rules of baseball state that only the catcher can be positioned in foul territory. Details, details.

BIGGEST BUMMERS

THE MOVE

On November 4, 1995, Cleveland area residents awoke to the *Plain Dealer* headline, "Browns Move in the Works." For days, rumors had been brewing about something happening with the Browns, and they came to a head on November 3 when Browns owner Art Modell suggested to reporters he was in serious negotiations with the city of Baltimore. Reporters asked Modell why he had broken his vow to never move the Browns as long as he owned the team. He replied, "As long as I owned the team, and as long as I was given any cooperation at all, that stood. As far as my proclamation that I would not move this team, that's gone, that's null and void because the game has changed considerably."

On November 6, 1995, Art Modell ascended a platform in a parking lot in downtown Baltimore to the cheers of "Art! Art! Art!" It was music to his ears, something he hadn't heard in Cleveland in a long time. Baltimore city officials and the state of Maryland bigwigs

Browns bolt
Modell warned mayor, governor a month ago

fawned over him as they made the most dreaded announcement in Cleveland sports—the Browns were moving to Baltimore. This act unleashed a frenzy not seen in modern day sports. Not only were the fans in Cleveland blind with rage, Browns fans all over the world climbed on the bandwagon of support for a city that had their beloved Browns stolen from them. Even the sports media community was outraged.

Former NFL player and coach Mike Ditka said, "Modell's actions were criminal. There was no team richer in tradition than the Cleveland Browns, but Modell destroyed it. If Modell were strapped for cash, he should have sold the Browns and gotten out of football. If he needed to feed his ego, this was the worst way to do it."

HE SHOULD HAVE SOLD THE BROWNS AND GOTTEN OUT OF FOOTBALL.

Bob Costas of NBC sports said, "Let's consider Art Modell. There's no doubt he's in debt. There's also no doubt that most of it is his fault. Remember, he bought the franchise for $4 million in the early 60s. It's now worth at least $160 million. He owned it through all the NFL's boom days of the '70s and '80s. And even in today's changed economic climate, the salary cap is $37 million, while each NFL team is guaranteed $38 million a year from network television alone. That's before they sell a single ticket or a bag of peanuts."

Bob Trumpy, the NBC commentator and former Cincinnati Bengals player who always had choice comments to make about Cleveland and the Browns when he announced Browns' games, came to the rescue. "I despise the whole concept of the Baltimore

Ravens. I wish the Ravens high winds and muddy fields; I wish them empty roads to and from the ballpark; I wish them cold hot dogs; I wish them nothing but bad."

Even hated Pittsburgh fans grieved the end of the Browns-Steelers rivalry and viewed the move of the franchise as an act of cowardice. As Matt Savrock, a lifelong Steelers fan, wrote in the Tulane newspaper, the *Hullabaloo*, "The Browns are not just Cleveland's loss; they are everyone's." Finally, the national media delivered a shot. *Sports Illustrated* covers are normally reserved for athletes, but on December 4, 1995, Art Modell appeared on the cover, though not in a way he would have liked. There in all its glory was an unflattering caricature of Art sucker punching a Browns' fan wearing a "Dawg" mask. Reportedly, Modell was furious over how he had been depicted. Normally, local Cleveland magazine distributors estimate 2,000 copies of *SI* are sold in a given week. The demand for this issue was near 50,000. Clevelanders from all walks of life were doing anything to show their outrage. Although the city received a new franchise in 1999, complete with the Browns' "name and colors," it could never be quite the same.

VINTAGE DIEKEN

Commenting on the move of the Cleveland Browns to Baltimore after the 1995 NFL season, former Browns player and then radio broadcaster Doug Dieken said, **"It's too sad even to be a country western song."**

THINK IT, JUST DON'T SAY IT

In the 2000 off season, Cavaliers General Manager Jim Paxson unloaded Shawn Kemp, the troublesome center, from the Cavs' roster. Then, Zydrunas Ilgauskas, the player they were counting on at center, was eliminated from the upcoming season with another foot injury. Paxson signed Bimbo Coles to a four-year deal, and Coles promptly had knee surgery. He traded for Matt Harpring, and Harpring had ankle surgery. On January 7, 2001, forward Lamond Murray said, **"I just don't know what it is here. I don't want to think about no curses, but you don't know what to think."** The next night, Murray had his cheekbone broken in a game against the New Jersey Nets.

BAD ⬤ TRADE

TOMMY AND TOMMIE

The Indians tried to make up for a huge mistake and only made things worse. On January 20, 1965, Tribe President Gabe Paul felt compelled to make a trade to help renew interest in Indians baseball. He re-acquired Rocky Colavito from the Kansas City Athletics in a three-team deal that saw Cleveland pitcher Tommy John, catcher John Romano, and outfielder Tommie Agee go to the Chicago White Sox. At the time, losing John did not seem significant because he had won only two games in two years for the Tribe. He performed well for the White Sox, going 82-80 over seven seasons. He was traded to the Los Angeles Dodgers in 1972, where he achieved fame for quite a different reason. After suffering a ruptured ligament in his left pitching elbow, John underwent radical surgery that successfully transplanted a section of ligament from his right arm into his left. The surgery became known as "Tommy John Surgery," and John went on to have a stellar pitching career with the Dodgers, New York Yankees, and California Angels, winning 288 games with 231 losses with a career earned run average of 3.34.

The other promising player sent to the White Sox was outfielder Tommie Agee, who saw limited big league action for Cleveland and then Chicago from 1962-1965, but blossomed in 1966 as the American League Rookie of the Year with a .273 batting average, 22 home runs and 86 runs batted-in. He is best known for his solid performance with the New York Mets and his defensive contributions to the "Amazin' Mets"

"WHAT A GRAB! TOMMIE AGEE!"

of 1969, when the underdog National League Champion won the World Series. "There's a deep drive to center . . . racing hard is Agee . . . What a grab! Tommie Agee!"

In trying to re-capture the mystique of the past, the Indians blundered by giving up good, young talent to re-acquire Colavito. Yet Rocky's presence in Cleveland for two and a half years helped stabilize a shaky franchise until new ownership came in 1967. Still, Tommy and Tommie would have looked good growing up in Indians' uniforms.

············ **ONLY IN CLEVELAND** ············

Duck!

During the 1966 season, Indians catcher Joe Azcue tried to throw out a base runner attempting to steal second base. The only problem was that his pitcher, Sonny Siebert, had turned away from the plate and was unaware of the throw. Azcue's peg down to second base hit Siebert in the back of his head. Siebert was not injured seriously, but the runner was safe.

CURSES!

AGONY OF DA FEET

Zydrunas Ilgauskas was playing basketball for the Atletas Basketball Club in Kaunas, Lithuania, in the 1994–1995 season and applied for entry into the NBA Draft in 1995. He withdrew his entry because he was forced to rehabilitate a broken right foot and missed the entire 1995–1996 season in Lithuania. But his entry into the 1996 NBA Draft resulted in the Cleveland Cavaliers selecting him with the twentieth pick in the first round. The word on Zydrunas was that he had all-star potential, good moves around the basket and, despite a thin frame, could bang under the boards when required. His weakness was soon exposed, however, and it wasn't his game on the court. He was plagued by chronic bone problems in both feet that caused multiple breaks. He nearly became another Cavaliers' first-round draft bust. Here are the "footnotes" to Ilgauskas' Cavaliers career:

1996–1997—Before the season started, Ilgauskas breaks his right foot again and surgery is performed on October 16, 1996. He misses the entire season.

1997–1998—In his first season in the NBA, Ilgauskas has a productive year, averaging 13.9 points per game and is selected to the NBA's All-Rookie First Team.

1998–1999—A labor dispute and NBA lockout of players postpones the start of the season until February 1999. Before the season is underway, the Cavs sign Ilgauskas to a new six-year contract for $71 million. He plays in the first five games of the season but fractures the navicular bone in his *left* foot.

1999–2000—Ilgauskas sits out the entire 1999–2000 season and continues to rehab his left foot. Further surgery is performed on his left foot on January 26, 2000.

2000–2001—A fresh start in 2000 sees Zydrunas start the first 24 games. On December 23, 2000, he removes himself from the game because of pain in his left foot. Surgery is performed and he misses the remainder of the season.

2001–2002—Continuing to rehab his left foot, Ilgauskas misses the first 17 games of the season but shows good progress in his play for the remainder of the year.

2002–2003—With his foot problems seemingly behind him, Ilgauskas plays in all 81 games.

2003–2004—Ilgauskas plays a full season.

2004–2005—Three full seasons in a row for "Big Z." After the season, the Cavs sign him to a new five-year contract in July 2005.

JUAN GONE

 Although a relatively inexpensive gamble, the Cleveland Indians signed outfielder and former two-time American League MVP Juan Gonzalez to a one-year $600,000 contract for the 2005 season. He yanked a hamstring muscle twice in spring training and was activated on May 31 for a game against the Minnesota Twins. On the third pitch of his first plate appearance, he pulled the muscle again trying to run to first base. That was pretty much it for the $600,000 they invested. The Indians should have taken a lesson from the Kansas City Royals, who'd had Gonzalez for the 2004 season. He appeared in only 33 games before being shelved by a disc problem in his lower back.

RUDD AS IN MUD

It was the first game of the 2002 NFL season for the Cleveland Browns and the Kansas City Chiefs. Cleveland's last home appearance on December 16, 2001 had been a national embarrassment as fans tossed plastic bottles on the field in protest of a referee's call that cost the Browns the game. But on September 8, 2002, it was, you guessed it, the referee's call that cost the Browns another home game. With 29 seconds left in the game, Phil Dawson had just kicked a field goal to put the Browns ahead 39-37. But holder Chris Gardocki was penalized for taunting the

Chiefs after the play. Penalized 15 yards, the Browns kicked off from their 15-yard line and the Chiefs returned it to their 35-yard line. At the 47-yard line, Kansas City quarterback Trent Green faced a first down with only four seconds left. Hoping to launch a prayer into the end zone, Green was apparently sacked by Cleveland linebacker Dwayne Rudd, sealing a Browns' victory. On his way to the ground, Green lateraled backward to offensive lineman John Tait, who lumbered down the sideline in front of a stunned Browns' bench. Tait was forced out of bounds and the game was over. Or was it?

Upfield, Rudd was doing some celebrating of his own, letting everyone in sold-out Browns Stadium know that he was "da-man." Referee Ron Blum joined in by tossing the yellow flag. He wasn't really objecting to Rudd's celebration so much as he didn't like Rudd's 15-yard helmet toss. He slapped him with an unsportsmanlike conduct penalty for removing his helmet on the field of play. Rudd was convinced he had brought Green to the ground and that the game was over. The penalty brought Kansas City to within their kicker's range. Morten Andersen booted the 33-yard field goal to win by one point. Rudd did admit that he should have kept his helmet on. But he also added that "we have 22 starters and it's a team game. One play didn't lose us this game." Oh, Dwayne . . . yes it did.

HE WAS "DA-MAN."

DIMINISHED SKILLS OR
DIMINISHED SENSE?

It was likened to the firing of Head Coach Paul Brown in 1963, and it rocked the football fans of Cleveland like nothing since. On November 8, 1993, the Cleveland Browns released the quarterback who nearly led them to the Super Bowl seven seasons earlier, and more importantly, the fan-favorite former college star who had actually maneuvered to play in his home town. Head Coach Bill Belichick and owner Art Modell cited the "diminishing skills" of the popular Bernie Kosar as the reason for dumping the Boardman, Ohio native.

The release may have had more to do with the nonrelationship between Belichick and Kosar. In a game against the Denver Broncos the day before his release, Kosar ran the offense by changing plays at the line of scrimmage and drawing up plays in the dirt. One of these went for a touchdown to wide receiver Michael Jackson—Kosar's last touchdown pass as a Brown. Reportedly, this was the last straw for Belichick. Modell told the media that in a meeting after the game, the coaching staff was unanimous in the decision to cut Kosar loose. Yet the Browns had signed Kosar to a six-year contract extension earlier in the season and named him the 1993 starting quarterback, because as Belichick said at the time, it gave the team its "best chance to win."

Quarterback Vinny Testaverde, who was signed at the start of the season to back-up Kosar, said, "I've watched Bernie since training camp and I don't think his skills have diminished, but it doesn't matter what I think." The theme

IT WAS TIME FOR THE TEAM TO MOVE ON AND RE-FOCUS.

coming from the Browns' offices was that Kosar, although charismatic, had never been the most athletic of field generals. Now, with injuries taking their toll, it was time for the team to move on and re-focus. That may have been a plausible explanation except for the fact that Art Modell said that Kosar's recent criticisms of the offense "have been a distraction that impacted negatively on the football team. We must protect the franchise and we want to get back into winning mode." In the following week's game against the Seattle Seahawks, the Browns said they were comfortable with reserve quarterback Todd Philcox at the controls (Vinny Testaverde was injured). Philcox fumbled his first snap from center. It was recovered by the Seattle defense and returned for a touchdown. The Browns lost 22-5. The Browns went on to lose six of their last eight games and finished the year at 7-9. While there was some merit to the assessment of Kosar's abilities, it was once again a question of style. An organization once known around the NFL as a class act had diminished itself in the way it chose to treat Bernie Kosar.

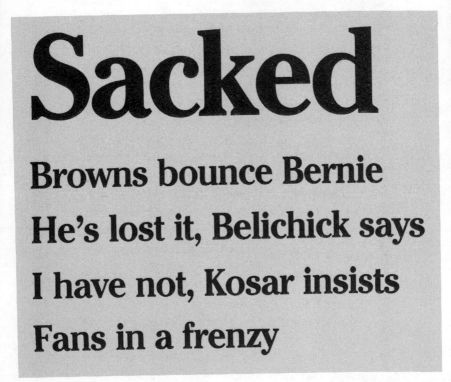

Sacked

Browns bounce Bernie

He's lost it, Belichick says

I have not, Kosar insists

Fans in a frenzy

BIGGEST BUMMERS

GAME SEVEN

October 26, 1997, looked like it would be etched in Cleveland Indians history as the date when half a decade's curse would be broken. The World Series against the Florida Marlins was knotted at three games apiece when Indians manager Mike Hargrove gave the seventh game start to rookie Jaret Wright over veteran Charles Nagy. Wright had beaten the Marlins in Game Four, and Hargrove felt comfortable starting the youngster over the veteran. As events unfolded, however, Nagy would be a part of this final game.

The Indians held a 2-0 lead until the Marlins' Bobby Bonilla homered in the bottom of the seventh inning. The game stayed at 2-1 until the bottom of the ninth, when Tribe's closer Jose Mesa took the hill. As cases of champagne were being iced in the Cleveland locker room, Mesa began showing signs of shakiness. First, the Marlins' Moises Alou singled, but Mesa was able to strike out Bonilla. Tribe fans everywhere were counting down the outs: a mere two more separated the Tribe from a World Series ring. Then Charles Johnson lined a single to right field, moving Alou to third. A Craig Counsell sacrifice fly to right scored the tying run. Mesa forced Jim Eisenreich to ground out for the third out, and it was in to extra innings.

The game was still deadlocked in the bottom of the eleventh inning when Bonilla singled off Charles Nagy, who had replaced Mesa. Gregg Zaun popped out, but then the whammy hit Cleveland when, once again, Craig Counsell's grounder went through second baseman Tony Fernandez for an error; Bonilla took third base. Eisenreich was intentionally walked to load the bases, but a Devon White grounder to Tony Fernandez forced out Bonilla at home. One more out was needed to keep the dream of a World Series alive, but Nagy couldn't get it. Edgar Rentaria

SURELY THE TRIBE WAS A TEAM OF DESTINY

hit a single to center field to score Counsell, and the Marlins became World Champs in just their fifth season of existence.

Surely the Tribe was a team of destiny that year, as they escaped

Just out of reach

certain doom in the playoffs against the Baltimore Orioles. But as the Marlins triumphed, there was a Florida fan holding a placard that read, "It's Our Turn." Give us a break . . . a World Championship in the franchise's fifth year! Don't the Indians get any points for being around ninety-six years? It was probably the bitterest loss in modern day Cleveland sports history, with a championship snatched away at the last minute. As Indians shortstop Omar Vizquel sat in the Cleveland clubhouse that had been prepared for a celebration with a TV stage and lights, he lamented, "You prepare your whole life for this. You dream about winning the World Series. Then this happens. It is a nightmare, just a nightmare."

DUBIOUS DRAFT

HE'S JUST A KID

In the 1996 NBA Draft, the Cavaliers selected 6'-10" center-forward Vitaly Potapenko, a native of Ukraine who played collegiate ball at Ohio's Wright State University. Vitaly was the twelfth pick in Round One. With the thirteenth pick, the Charlotte Hornets selected a young high school phenom from Lower Merion High School in Philadelphia by the name of Kobe Bryant. He was *USA Today* and *Parade* magazine's 1996 National High School Player of the Year. The Hornets traded Bryant to the Los Angeles Lakers for center Vlade Divac before the start of the 1996–1997 season. A seven-time NBA All-Star, Bryant helped lead the Los Angeles Lakers to three consecutive NBA titles in 2000, 2001, and 2002 and is considered by many pro basketball analysts to be one of the most talented players in the league today. Potapenko played just over two seasons with the Cavaliers and was traded to the Boston Celtics on March 11, 1999, and later joined the Seattle Supersonics as a back-up center-forward.

FROM THE PENTHOUSE TO THE OUTHOUSE

The 2004–2005 Cleveland Cavaliers looked like they had the makings of a playoff team. It was the second NBA season for "Chosen One" Lebron James. As fans peeked at the standings in the Eastern Conference Central Division in mid-January, the Cavaliers were not out of it; in fact, they were sitting on top with a 22-13 record, leading the Detroit Pistons by a half game. As February came, they held the same edge over Detroit. But February was not kind to the Cavs as they went 5-7, slipped into second place,

IN FACT, THEY WERE SITTING ON TOP WITH A 22-13 RECORD

and trailed the Pistons on March 1 by five games. They lost their last three games in February and dropped their first three in March.

If losing weren't tough enough, an ownership change on March 1 didn't exactly foster the image of a confident playoff-bound organization. Michigan mortgage loan millionaire, Dan Gilbert, bought the Cavs for $375 million from George and Gordon Gund and three weeks later fired head coach Paul Silas and replaced him with assistant coach Brendan Malone. The team was now reeling from the turmoil and it showed in a 6-9 March record. The Cavs lost two games by 19 points and one by 31 points in the aftermath of Silas' firing. By April 1 they sported a 37-34 record and had fallen to third place, seven and a half games behind the Pistons. On April 17, the Cavaliers lost to the Pistons by

No playoffs for Cavs

three points. Lebron James, as was his role in the last month of the season, attempted to win the game single handedly. He missed a 30-foot jumper at the end of the game and showed his disgust by separating himself from his Cavs jersey as he left the floor. While the Cavs owned James's rights for an additional three years, the *Plain Dealer*'s Bill Livingston wrote on the day after the Cavs season ended, "Without substantial improvement, he (James) sheds the uniform for keeps after that." What seemed like such a promising season as late as mid-February turned into a 42-40 fourth place finish.

POPPING WHEELIES

One would think that if you're a first-round pick in the NFL draft with a $40 million contract containing incentives *and* you're rehabilitating a broken leg from the season before, you might not want to risk further harm to yourself. But when you're young, stupid, and have millions in the bank, what's wrong with enjoying yourself? To Kellen Winslow, Jr., the Browns' rookie tight end, a fascination with high-powered motorcycles nearly cost him his career and endangered his life. On May 1, 2005, one day after the Browns completed a rookie mini-camp, Winslow went to a deserted parking lot in Westlake, Ohio to practice riding his Suzuki GSX-R750 motorcycle with other cyclists. During his stint in the parking lot, Winslow lost control of his bike and hit a curb. He knocked over a four-foot shrub and landed in an area of tree branches. When EMS technicians arrived, Winslow was still on the ground complaining of chest pain and having difficulty breathing. His helmet had flown off during the fall because it was not fastened properly. Winslow was treated for internal injuries and experienced swelling in his shoulder and right knee.

The consensus among cycle professionals was that the Browns'

Winslow injured in accident

rookie had way too much bike under him as an unskilled cyclist. The bike Winslow purchased, known as "gixxer" on the streets, was a popular model with riders seeking speed. The final injury toll was a lacerated liver and kidney, bruised shoulder, cracked thigh bone, and a torn anterior cruciate ligament in the right knee. On June 14, Winslow had the torn ligament surgically repaired with the verdict that he would not see the football field in 2005. Winslow stood to loose a lot of money because he violated the terms of his agreement that prohibited certain hazardous activities, but the Browns "re-worked" Winslow's contract, giving him the opportunity to earn back his lost compensation over time.

The media circus that surrounded Winslow, his father (former NFL receiver Kellen Winslow, Sr.) and Junior's agents, the famed Poston brothers, Kevin and Keith, was pure theater. Some of Winslow Sr.'s rants to the media were precious. "You guys look at this as a moment in time and you blow it out of proportion. This Jerry Springer mentality of journalism, you guys are better than that. You should be ashamed of yourselves. Presidents make mistakes. Senators make mistakes. Journalists, if you still call yourselves that, make mistakes." But in this case Kellen Winslow Jr. made the mistake; he just wasn't ready to admit it.

THE BROWNS' ROOKIE HAD **WAY TOO MUCH BIKE** UNDER HIM.

CURSES!

SUPER JOE

On December 6, 1978, the Cleveland Indians sent little-known pitcher Cardell Camper to the Philadelphia Phillies for little-known Joe Charboneau. Charboneau was immediately sent to the Tribe's Class AA farm team in Chattanooga, Tennessee but soon slugged his way to the big leagues by hitting .352 and 21 home runs in the minors. Indians manager Dave Garcia put him in the lineup on Opening Day in 1980, and Charboneau proceeded to hit a home run, double, and a single to start on the road toward the American League Rookie of the Year Award, which he won with a .289 batting average, 23 home runs, and 87 runs batted in. Joe also earned the nickname, "Super Joe," that was accompanied by a song:

Who's the newest guy in town?
Go Joe Charboneau!
Turns the ballpark upside down.
Go Joe Charboneau!

Who's the one to keep our hopes alive
Straight from seventh to the pennant drive
Raise your glass, let out a cheer
For Cleveland's Rookie of the Year!

Charboneau's book, *Super Joe: The Life and Legend of Joe Charboneau*, was written with sportswriters Terry Pluto and Burt Graeff and there were plenty of legends to tell. Joe reportedly had swallowed six cigarettes to win a $5 bet, ate a shot glass, boxed bare-fisted and bare-chested in a boxcar to win $30, opened beer bottles with his eye-socket, and extracted his own teeth. Fans in Cleveland couldn't get enough of him because he provided weary Indians' fans with a much-needed tonic—both on and off the field.

Alas, during spring training in 1981, Super Joe became just a regular Joe. First a groin injury, then back problems, and perhaps a smattering of the dreaded sophomore jinx brought Joe crashing back to earth. In only 48 games, Charboneau hit .210 with 4 home runs and 18 runs batted-in. He was sent back to the minor leagues but the 1982 season saw him play in only 22 big league games for Cleveland, after which he was released. In early February 1984, he signed as a free agent with the Pittsburgh Pirates but didn't stick. Eventually he found himself playing sandlot baseball in Buffalo, New York,

ESPN.COM LISTS CHARBONEAU AT NUMBER TWO ON ITS LIST OF BASEBALL'S ONE-HIT WONDERS.

but never made it back to the big leagues. ESPN.com lists Charboneau at number two on its list of baseball's one-hit wonders. For one crazy year, Cleveland basked in the promise of a fabled young hotshot who became the Rookie of the Year. Not bad for a guy who once got drunk, woke up with a tattoo, and then used a razor blade to remove it. Ah, Joe, we hardly knew ye!

THE FIZZLE

First they get your hopes up . . .

In 2005, after a lackluster first half, the Tribe went on a surprising tear in August and September, lighting the fuse for what promised to be a sizzling rocket ride toward the postseason. Alas, the sizzle turned to fizzle when the team's hot young hitters turned cold in the final week of the season. The Indians dropped five of their last six games (including two of three to the mediocre Tampa Bay Devil Rays). On the last day of the season, they ran out of gas just one game short of the playoffs.

As late as the end of July, the Indians were lodged firmly in third place, 14½ games behind the Chicago White Sox. Then the Tribe rallied for a 19-8 August record and cut the White Sox lead in half by month's end. As the Sox stumbled in September, the Indians surged. Between September 1 and September 19, the team racked up an impressive 13-3 record. They trailed the Sox by only 2½ games heading into the Windy City for a three-game series. There, emboldened by their recent success, they took two of three. They were now just 1½ games behind the White Sox—and leading in the AL Wild Card race by a game.

Things were getting interesting. National media flocked to the games. There was talk of Eric Wedge winning the American League Manager of the Year Award, and Travis Hafner was being touted as a legitimate MVP candidate. Fans back in Cleveland started getting that gleam in their eyes, and an "anything can happen" mood began to creep into Cleveland's collective consciousness.

Yes, anything can happen. Unfortunately.

The Indians' nosedive began on the afternoon of Sunday, September 25, when they lost to the Kansas City Royals 5-4. In a tight race, a close loss is disappointing. But the way the Indians lost this game left many fans whistling by the graveyard.

The game was deadlocked 4-4, the Royals batting in the last of the ninth inning. With a runner on second base, KC's Paul Phillips hit a shot to center field toward Tribe outfielder Grady Sizemore. "It was right at me," Sizemore said later. "It just got in the sun. I knew it was going to be in the sun. I tried to wait for it to come out and I just never saw it." The ball deflected off Sizemore's hip, and when he didn't react quickly

"EVEN WHEN THE SUN IS SHINING BRIGHTEST ON A CLEVELAND TEAM, ANGST CREEPS IN."

enough to pick it up and throw it home, the Royals scored and the game was over.

The next day in the Plain Dealer, Bud Shaw wrote what many

fans in Cleveland didn't want to consider. "Even when the sun is shining brightest on a Cleveland team, angst creeps in." Waxing prophetically, Shaw continued. "Black cats, broken mirrors and baseballs lost in the sun fall into the same general category for those expecting something to go amiss for the Indians in the final week of the season."

Go amiss things did.

What transpired over the next week can be filed under Pitiful in the annals of Cleveland sports history. The pesky Devil Rays darted into Jacobs Field and took the first two games by one run. Now four games behind Chicago, the Indians had no hope of winning the Central Division. It was win the Wild Card or pack your bags as the White Sox came to town for the final three games of the season. The Tribe had excellent pitching but could no longer hit. What baserunners they had, they squandered. After living by the home run for the past two months, they died in a power failure. The Sox swept, 3-2, 4-3, and 3-1, and Cleveland's season was through.

Indians' pitcher C.C. Sabathia observed, "I know these chances don't come along often. And I don't want to jinx myself. But I feel I'm going to get a lot more of these chances at the postseason with this team." The last thing Cleveland wants is another jinx, C.C. !

Oh, by the way: who was featured on the cover of the October 3, 2005 issue of Sports Illustrated? The Indians' own Ronnie Belliard. Thought you'd like to know.

The cave-in is is complete

CURSES!

YOU NAME IT:

Have we covered everything?

Maybe so. Hey—maybe this is the end of trail . . . no more dud draft picks or dumb trades. No more flameouts. No more curses. No more heart-wrenching defeats. Maybe the Browns, Cavs, and Tribe will now get our hopes up, only to . . . to . . . charge on into championship glory!

Well, we can dream, can't we?

Meanwhile, here's some space in which you can jot down the next installments in the ongoing chronicles of Cleveland sports woe. Let's hope it's enough space to last a couple of years . . .